First Church of the Brethren
1340 Forge Road
Carlisle, Pennsylvania 17013

ONE WAY TO CHANGE THE WORLD

ONE WAY

TO CHANGE

THE WORLD

LEIGHTON FORD

HARPER & ROW, PUBLISHERS

NEW YORK, EVANSTON, AND LONDON

1817

LIBRARY OF CONGRESS CATALOG CARD NUMBER: 71-124701

CONTENTS

PREFACE

In September 1969 the U. S. Congress on Evangelism was held in Minneapolis. I was asked by the committee to speak to the issue of evangelism in a day of revolution. During my preparation of that address I began to see clearly that as believers we could take one of three basic positions toward the change and revolution convulsing our world. We could try to ignore change; we could fear and resist it; or we could seek to guide it.

I was gripped with the conviction that God is calling us to that last option, that He wants us to be part of the world struggle—with no superhuman pretensions, with no illusions as to what "success" might be ours—but in partnership with the Christ Who is the true revolutionary.

At the Congress I tried to share these convictions. There was a sense of its being the right word in the right place at the right time—in other words, God's word, His place, His time. I believe, quite simply, that God spoke in a way beyond what I was capable of doing. The response was immediate and continuing. Many delegates voiced their kindred longing for an evangelism that would be both unquestionably rooted in the unchanging Gospel and realistically related to a changing world.

From that address has grown this book. Those who read the former will recognize some of the material. But here I have expanded and further illustrated a number of points.

A word about the title is in order. There is a remarkable movement on the U. S. West Coast known as "evangelical hippies." Hundreds, perhaps thousands, of young people have been converted to Christ from the hippie, drug and radical countercultures. When other young people flash the two-finger "peace" signal, these Christian youth give their own signal—the raised index finger—meaning "*One* Way, *One* Way"—that Christ is God's one way for man. It is in this sense that the title should be taken. Not "one way" among others to change the world. But the *only* way that will work.

Acknowledgments are always in order. Here the gratitude goes beyond the words. Thanks to my wife, Jeanie, always encouraging, warm, interested; to my "boss" and colleague, Billy Graham, who has been responsive and understanding; to my close friend of many years, Calvin Thielman, minister of the Presbyterian Church, Montreat, North Carolina, who painstakingly worked over the Minneapolis address with me; to Norman Pell, director of my Crusades; to Howard Jones, Associate Evangelist with Billy Graham, who gave helpful comments on various points; and to my tireless secretary, Leola Linkous, who typed the many revisions.

—LEIGHTON FORD

Charlotte, North Carolina
August 1970

1 THIS IS THE WORLD THAT WAS

In London's Highgate Cemetery a huge granite pillar stands on top of the grave of Karl Marx. On it sits a bust of Marx, his cheeks puffed out like Kris Kringle, his eyes set deep and resolute. Chiseled on the granite is this dictum of the father of Communism: "The philosophers have only interpreted the world in various ways; the point however is to change it."

Christians agree with Karl Marx! The world does need to be changed. But to what end, and how? That is the point.

The Christian church is being called today to evangelize a world in the grip of revolution. But what has evangelism to do with revolution? Just this: that Christ's work never goes on in a vacuum. The biblical faith sees that God is moving amid the events of real history. Luke claimed to write his account of Jesus as a careful historian (Luke 1:1-4). It is significant that he carefully connects the facts about Jesus with the facts of the "secular" world. He notes that Jesus was born at the time of Caesar Augustus' decree that all the world should be enrolled, and he specifically points out that this was the first enrollment when Quirinius was governor of Syria (Luke 2:1-2). He pinpoints the beginning of John the Baptist's ministry during "the fifteenth year of the reign of Tiberius Caesar, Pontius Pilate being governor of Judaea, and Herod being tetrarch of Galilee . . ." (Luke 3:1). That would be like dating a contemporary event as happening when Richard Nixon was President of the United States, Nelson Rockefeller Governor of New York State, and John Lindsay Mayor of New York City. Luke is making the point that in Jesus Christ God came into a real world of real people with a real history. Similarly, evangelism will not be effective if we ignore the realities of the world in which we make our witness. And the cataclysmic revolutionary movements of our time involve the very people for whom

1

Christ died and toward whom our evangelism is directed.

This truth was smashed into my heart in Africa nearly a decade ago when a friend and I were flying from Ghana to the Congo. Ghana had recently gained its freedom; the Congo was to receive independence a few months later. Africa was throbbing with the great drive for freedom; the thunder of change was in the air. My friend was reading his Bible and quietly handed it to me, pointing to this passage from Jeremiah:

The word of the Lord came to me . . . saying, "What do you see?" And I said, "I see a boiling pot, a seething cauldron—facing away from the north." Then the Lord said to me, "Out of the north evil shall break forth upon all the inhabitants of the land. For, lo, I am calling all the tribes of the kingdoms of the north . . . against all the cities of Judah. And I will utter my judgments against them, for all their wickedness in forsaking me" (Jeremiah 1:13–16).

"A seething cauldron." That picture seemed to describe perfectly the Africa and the world of our day, shaken and convulsed by the most fantastic revolutions of all time. When the mobs stormed the Bastille in 1789 to start the French Revolution, King Louis XVI is said to have remarked, "This is a revolt." Someone replied, "No, sir, this is a revolution." Indeed, this is also the mark of our age, not an isolated revolt but total revolution.

Strictly speaking, the word "revolution" means total or radical change. There was a revolution when industry switched from muscle power to machine power; when astronomy changed its viewpoint from an earth-centered to a sun-centered universe; when politics shifted from the divine right of kings to the Magna Charta and the Bill of Rights; when society moved from slavery to freedom.

More broadly, revolution is the pattern of change—total, constant, irresistible, rapid, pervasive—that affects every part of our lives. There are many dimensions to this wholesale change that is going on. One aspect is the so-called demographic revolution, the worldwide population explosion. According to World Health Organization figures, 3.7 human beings are born every second. This totals some 221 per minute, 318,575 per day, and more than 2.2 million per week. At this rate, the world population, which now stands at around 3.5 billion, is expected to reach nearly 7 billion in the next three decades. Historian Arnold Toynbee has warned that "if we have a nuclear war, too few people will be left alive to maintain civilization; if we do not, too many people will make life on this planet intolerable." Ecologists today sound like new Jeremiahs crying that the earth's shrinking resources will not sustain its bursting billions.

Runaway population growth must be of concern to the Christian cause, in terms of both compassion for human suffering and our commitment to evangelism. It has been estimated that in spite of the combined efforts of all churches and evangelistic and missionary agencies put together it is taking 1000 Christians an average of 365 days to win one person to Christ. This is not good enough!

There is some measure of disagreement among researchers as to how the Christian cause is doing in proportion to the rapidly expanding world population. The 1968 *World Christian Handbook* maintains that at the present spiritual growth rate, during the rest of this century Christianity will expand only one-third as rapidly as the whole world's population. A German mission official, Heinrich Lohmann, is pessimistic. In the next twenty-five years, he asserts, Christian influence in the world will be cut in half. By the year 2000, he says, only 15% of the world population will be even nominally Christian. On the other hand, Dr. David Barrett, perhaps the most informed researcher in the world on this subject, takes a different view. In spite of the growing number of non-Christians, he holds that by A.D. 2000 the proportion of Christians in the world will be at 31%, slightly higher than it was in 1900. Regardless of which view is right, we must realize that our evangelistic task has only just begun.

In America the demographic revolution is especially marked by huge population shifts, great slides of humanity. By 1980 the Christian church will find its evangelistic mission focused on the 90% of all Americans who will live in great strip cities, already dubbed with such revolting names as Boswash, Chipitt, and Sansan (denoting the population corridors from Boston to Washington, from Chicago to Pittsburgh, and from San Franciso to San Diego). A church that cannot effectively relate its gospel to urban man is inviting decline and extinction. Although we blandly assume that the Bible relates to sheep and green grass, these rural metaphors are balanced in the Scripture by compassion for the city.

Our Lord chose Jerusalem as a prime target. It is recorded that He wept twice: once over the death of His friend Lazarus and once over the death of the city that rejected Him. Paul based his missionary strategy in the key cities of his day. He chose to stay in Ephesus for two years, using it as a sounding board from which the Gospel could spread through the surrounding province. He had a restless longing to declare in Rome, the nerve center of his day, the same message he had made known in Jerusalem and Athens. John saw God's future order coming down from Heaven, not as a garden but as a holy city! If only we could learn to reread our Bibles with contemporized eyes, we might overcome our tendency to assume that God's work can be seen in the Grand Canyon but not on Wall Street or at the corner of Hollywood and Vine.

We also live in a blindingly fast technological revolution. The "application gap" has shrunk amazingly. It is estimated that from the discovery of the telegraph until its commercial application it took 112 years; for telephone it took 56 years; for radio 34 years; for radar 15; for television 12; for atomic power 6; and for transistors only 5 years. Our exploding technology is like all the rockets at Cape Kennedy going off at once in some Fourth of July spectacular!

Yet the advance of technology is a mixed blessing. Witness men on the moon versus pollution in our lakes! As Dr. Emmanuel Mesthene, director of the Program on Technology and Society at Harvard University, says, "we can explore the heavens . . . or destory the world. We can cure disease or poison entire populations. We can free enslaved millions or enslave millions more." Since technology and science are morally neutral, Dr. Mesthene goes on to point out that "its massive power can lead to massive error so efficiently perpetrated as to be well nigh irreversible." Yet to ask whether technology is good or bad is in a sense beside the point. It is like asking whether a great rushing river is good or bad. The fact is that it's here and it's moving and we have to learn to live with it.

The strange plight of modern man is that while his knowledge is exploding, the whole idea of "true truth," truth that is the opposite of falsehood, is disappearing. Modern man is seeking to "escape from reason." In art, in philosophy, in theology, and in the total pattern of his thinking relativism is the rule. Nothing is certain. The modern mind has shifted into neutral, producing a cult of relativity and nonmeaning. In nearly every field of study we can see what Professor Dirk Jellema of the Case Institute has called "the post-modern mind." Relativism is seen in the philosophy of Thomas Dewey in education, of Albert Einstein in physics, of Oliver Wendell Holmes in jurisprudence. Existentialism, following after logical positivism, denies that we can express anything meaningful about God. The psychiatrists now tell us that no one is really "on"; the question is, "How far off are you?" There is universal suspicion for any message that claims authority.

"Do your own thing," the phrase popularized by the hippies, fits the mood of our day like a glove. It's your life. Don't let anyone else tell you how to run it. You make the decisions. You call the shots. In one sense this attitude is healthy, for each of us is an individual. Each of us has certain God-given rights and gifts and we can't fit into somebody else's mold. But at another level this "Do your own thing" mind-set becomes almost sinister. It has become a symbol of the revolt against authority. Today society is being ripped apart by the tension between anarchy on the one hand and authoritarianism on the other.

A state of "anarchy" is simply one without a ruler. It is nothing new. Back in the days of the Judges the Bible records that ". . . there was no king in Israel; every man did what was right in his own eyes' (Judges 17:6). For some people anarchy has become a total way of life. Picture a hippie sitting cross-legged in his pad, wearing his beads and smoking his pot. He has dropped out of what he regards as being "straight" society. He is trying to "do his own thing." He has rejected all the things he thinks society is trying to impose on him. He is a kind of gentle, mild-mannered anarchist.

On the other extreme are the yippies, or the militant anarchists. The radical Left among students actually wants to do away with all government, all structure, and all authority. During the riots in Paris more rioters carried the black flag of anarchy than carried the red flag of Communism. British pop singer Mick Jagger, a member of the "Rolling Stones," was arrested for possessing drugs illegally.

At his trial he said, "It's when authority won't allow something that I dig in. I am against anything that interferes with individual freedom. As a nonconformist I won't accept what other people say is right and there are hundreds like me, thousands."

The hippies and the yippies are just the dramatic fringes of an anarchy that pervades every facet of life. Sometimes it seems that everything that's been nailed down is coming loose. An educator observes that "on university and college campuses authority is virtually a swear word."

In the home many parents are afraid to say "no" to their children. It is interesting that a Louis Harris poll taken for *Life* magazine indicated there is almost unanimous criticism of the lack of discipline in the family. Not only did the pollsters find that young and old agree (by 79%) that parental influence has declined over the past ten years, but 53% of the teenagers and 75% of the young adults thought that "parents have become too permissive." An outstanding 74% of teenagers and 88% of young adults agreed that "parents spoil their kids today." If these attitudes are maintained the next generation may find itself in for an old-fashioned upbringing. Nevertheless, now the revolt against authority is in full stride. Students protest the right of college and university authorities to make rules governing their personal behavior. The most authoritarian religious groups are finding that their total control over their followers is coming unglued.

Questioning authority is not new. Nor is it entirely without merit, for to some extent it's part of growing up. The very word "exist" means "to stand out from." The young person who is trying to find out who he is has to stand out from others, to question authority to some extent, and even on occasion to buck authority when it's wrong. Within limits, God has set things up to change through this natural process. But today's problem is that the revolution against reason has left us without any standards. It's not just that the traditional authorities may sometimes be wrong. It's that there is no final authority.

Inevitably this has led to a moral revolution, a shift from an absolute ethic to a situation ethic, from a morality based on God's eternal law to one based on man's personal likes. One college student is quoted as having said, "The only absolute in the universe is the speed of light." Another asserted, "I try to follow three of the ten commandments—some of the time!" Or as a coed put it, "I know what I think is right and wrong, but I'm not telling anyone else what to do."

This surface confusion reflects deep uncertain tides underneath. Intellectual and moral upheavals have carried many people all the way from a rigid and irrelevant authoritarianism to an unbuttoned anarchy. Few ever consider whether there is a real and genuine authority in which we can find both true freedom and true responsibility.

All these changes are compounded by the communications revolution that has both shrunk this planet into one world and extended our eyes to the moon. Most first-graders have already watched television for more hours than they will ever sit in a college classroom! The immediacy of the media has placed us all in what Marshall McLuhan calls a "global village." An American couple watches their son gunned down in Southeast Asia, courtesy of the relay satellite. News today is not just what's happened; it's what's happening!

The children of the electronic age are the first generation ever to know more than their parents! When young people say that those over thirty don't understand they may be arrogant, but they are also partly right. Most of the changes mentioned here have taken place in the last thirty years. It's estimated that 60% of our current usable information has been discovered or changed since World War II. Those of us born before 1939 are like immigrants, feeling our way around a new land. This is what Margaret Mead means when she says that only the young know this world as natives know their own country. Change is the natural habitat of today's youth.

We are living through a revolution of the young. Robert Kennedy once suggested that the world is engaged in a "war in the fourth dimension—the dimension of time—and the future belongs to whoever can capture the minds and wills and imaginations of the young."

One morning several years ago I stood in Seoul, Korea, and watched Army troops and trucks maneuvering. When I asked my guide if they were afraid of an invasion from the Communists to the North he said, "No, we're not afraid of the Communists, we're afraid of the students. They overthrew the government last year and we're afraid they will do it again." The following Sunday afternoon I was in Tokyo. As a friend and I walked through the city we saw little knots of young people gathering, arguing, debating, making signs, and singing. Within what seemed like just a few minutes 5000 of them were marching down the streets of Tokyo, protesting against a treaty their government was about to sign. At Red Square in the Kremlin Billy Graham saw thousands of Communist youth chanting, "We're going to change the world, we're going to change the world." In Communist China literally millions of young people read, memorize, and live by the thoughts of Chairman Mao, written in a little red book, and worship their Chairman as their lord and savior.

These young adults remind us that revolution also means radical political change. We are all heirs of the revolutions that have shaped our world. The United States has not yet reached the 200th anniversary of its Revolution. We stand only 180 years from the thud of the guillotine in France. And in historian Alan Morehead's words, the Russian Revolution of 1917 (an event that, he says, "means almost as much to the devoted Communist as the resurrection of Christ means to the Christian") triggered an "explosion that still rocks the world."

A few years ago the prospect of revolution seemed very remote on the North American Continent. How many of us ever thought we would live to see a revolution here? Yet today the extremist groups in our society call for just that.

In these days, when "revolution" is a word so loosely used, it is important to distinguish between revolutions and revolutions. The American Revolution was a revolution with particular and limited goals. In contrast, the French and Communist revolutions rejected totally the ancient regimes and created new ones that were in many ways worse. What today's radicals have in mind for America is much closer to the French than to the American Revolution.

While both the American and French revolutionaries held up the ideals of individual liberty and equality, in France there was countenanced the Reign of Terror, when tens of thousands of

Frenchmen were guillotined. Even worse, that Revolution cut freedom away from its foundations of faith. The Dutch theologian and politician Abraham Kuyper pointed out years ago that to understand the French Revolution one must grasp both its necessity and its sin. In *Christianity and the Class Struggle* he says,

The French Revolution was indeed a righteous judgment of God on those who had misused the authority and power entrusted to them. But this in no way lessens the deeply sinful character of this French Revolution, insofar as . . . it substituted the will of the *individual* for the will of the *Creator* of nations . . . while it brought a breathing spell, simultaneously [it] brought the seed of a corruption which is now deadlier than the corruption they revolted against in 1789.

The ruthlessness, violence, and suppression that have been spawned by the Communist revolutions are also agonizingly fresh in our minds.

Our current extremists have a vision akin to that of the French and Communist revolutionaries. Radicals in the Western world today have made their goal clear: they are convinced that society is so corrupt and so unworkable that the system cannot be changed—it must be destroyed. When asked what they have to replace it, many of them answer that this is not their concern. It should be ours, for they are out to create a vacuum that would quickly be filled by the totalitarianism of either the left or the right.

Yet we dare not be blind to the lessons all modern revolutions have taught: when men of privilege abuse their power, and when justice and reform are refused, sooner or later upheaval will come. President John F. Kennedy put it memorably, "He who makes peaceful revolution impossible makes violent revolution inevitable."

Today revolution is fueled by the freedom drive that is surging up through the entire world of man—the struggle for identity, dignity, security, and equality.

On the world scene one cannot understand revolution without taking into account the force of national pride. Arnold Toynbee asserts that "nationalism is about ninety per cent of the religion of about ninety per cent of mankind." Many good things can be said in favor of nationalism, but we must remember that it can become a false religion, demand the supreme loyalty of men, and become the chief competitor to the Lordship of Christ.

The emerging nations of the Third World are also caught in the "revolution of rising expectations," the phrase coined by Adlai Stevenson to describe their hunger for food, for health, for housing, and for a piece of the twentieth century. This planet is indeed a "lopsided world," where the rich get richer and the poor get poorer.

In America the flash points of the freedom revolution are poverty and racism. The poor have always been with us but the gap yawns wider every year. The new factor is that poor people are learning that not everyone is poor and that change is possible. Put television in a ghetto, let a slum mother see ads for low-calorie dog foods and electric toothbrushes when her baby has had its ears chewed off by a rat, and you've got the making of a revolution!

Racism is not just a problem of the southern states or of America or of the white man. It is a worldwide symptom of sin. But God has told us to confess our own sins, not those of the rest of the world. All over the world men of every color are fighting for equality and dignity. When a man loses hope he goes mad, and the violence of despair that has erupted in the great cities of North America and other parts of the world tells us in searing terms that the revolution is here. If our reaction as Christians is simply to lash back, and if we do not try to heal the gaping, aching, rubbed-raw wounds of racial strife, then we shall deserve the fire next time.

Too commonly we Christians throw up our hands in horror when we look at the revolutions of our world. Have we stopped to think that when we as Christians preach the Gospel we are in a sense sowing the seeds of revolution? The rights of men to freedom, dignity, and respect come directly from the Bible, from the story that God made man and God loves man and that the Son of God laid down His life for man. This is the ultimate source of human worth. The "revolution of rising expectations" can also be traced back to Christian influence. Modern science developed in the West, where Christianity had taught the reality and goodness of the material world, not in the East, where the major religions denied material reality. The whole idea that the course of history can be altered, that man is not the slave of fate, comes from the Christian view that history moves toward a climax; this is in contrast with those philosophies that for centuries taught people that history was a cycle repeating itself endlessly.

It is too late, then, for us Christians to contract out. We are in some sense the agents of change. The question is: What should be the stance of the Christian church in an age of revolution?

2 THE CHRISTIAN'S STANCE

Picture a monk in a quiet cloister, hands folded in prayerful meditation. Picture a rioter at the barricades, holding a Molotov cocktail in one hand and a submachine gun in the other. These two extremes characterize the deep split in the Christian church today.

Christians have been polarizing in their reaction to a changing world and it sometimes seems that these two caricatures are the only options open to us, to be monks in retreat or to be guerrilla fighters on attack. Some call for the blind rejection of all revolution; others demand a naïve acceptance of all revolution. Some would like to ignore change; others would like to baptize change as the new Messiah. Some would respond to revolution by trying to dig in and stop change; others would try to change the Gospel and make Jesus into the patron saint of guerrilla fighters. As responsible Christians we must reject both extremes.

We cannot be worthy of our high calling if we try to keep God in some private undisturbed corner of our lives and ignore the strong driving winds of change. If we are satisfied with the status quo, happy to put huge amounts of money into buildings used only a few hours a week, content to continue the same old programs in the same old ways on a strictly limited basis while the devilish forces go full blast 24 hours a day; willing to spend our time in petty quarrels over details of eschatology while millions have never heard the great truths of the Good News: more jealous of our denominational progress than of the spread of the Gospel; more concerned to debate personalities than to declare Christ—then we will be like Rip Van Winkle, who slept through a revolution and woke to find pictures of President George instead of King George in the taverns.

While revolution was raging in Petrograd in 1917, the Russian Orthodox church was in session a few blocks away reportedly having a warm debate about what color vestments their priests should wear! God help us if we strain at gnats while the camels of revolution are marching! God give us courage to be like the prophets who climbed their watchtowers to see what God was doing in the world. Jesus told us to "watch"—to be alert, to discern the "signs of the times." "Let us not sleep as others do," exhorted Paul, "but let us keep awake and be sober." God expects us to evangelize with our eyes wide open!

Some change should be opposed. As Christians we have a stake in preserving the historic truth of the Gospel and the worthy values of the past. Like Jeremiah we say, "Ask for the ancient paths, where the good way is." In that sense we are conservatives. But we also know that sin infects every man and every human institution, so we need a holy discontent with the status quo. The Gospel calls for constant change. Conversion is a change of direction; repentance is a change of mind. And the Christian life is a continual change from glory to glory. In that sense we are radicals.

We cannot identify our Gospel with the past and oppose all change. Personally, I don't find it comfortable to change. I like my old shoes and my old sermons, but I find that God won't let me settle down comfortably. He urges me on, for God is not tied to 17th-century English, 18th-century hymns, 19th-century architecture, and 20th-century clichés. To be sure, our faith does offer security with everything else changing. But when I am uptight and defensive it's often because I've forgotten the dynamic, neverending, exciting process of change that I got involved in when I got involved with Jesus Christ. If any man is in Christ he is a new creature, says my Bible, and not only has the old passed away but all things are becoming new! Here we have no continuing city. God is constantly prodding us as He did the people of Israel, saying, "Strike your tents and move on!"

The naïve approval of revolution is an equally foolish mistake. A spokesman for the Black Christ movement claims that Jesus came to lead a black Israel struggling for liberation and that He was basically a nationalistic revolutionary. He was crucified because He fought against white oppression. Probably very few black or white Christians would swallow this (though we ought to realize that a black Jesus is no more incongruous than a blonde, blue-eyed Jesus, for He was actually a swarthy Jew).

There have been many attempts to recast Jesus into the role of a political revolutionary, the "pale socialist" of Galilee. Some religious leaders see the church's task today as being "the handmaiden or waterboy of the world revolution." They have picked revolution as the wave of the future and they are trying to ride it. One theologian lists the various changes going on in the world and concludes, "God is in all these revolutions." Another asserts, "Change is the way the God of justice shatters an unjust order and opens up the way of God's world for justice."

I think it is fair to reply, "How do you know?" How can one tell whether it is God or the devil at work in revolution? Jesus described a house from which one demon was cast out and seven more came in. A revolution that takes place in a spiritual vacuum will open the door wide for the invasion of demons!

Communism is a prime example of the demonic possibilities in revolution. Certainly we should be wary of efforts to identify evangelism with a crude, sword-rattling anti-Communism. Instead, we've got to love the Communist: to acknowledge the injustice that has been the seedbed for Communism, to try to understand the appeal that Communism has to many students and intellectuals, and to resist the temptation to blame all our problems on the Communists.

Yet we cannot blind ourselves to the brutalities that have marked the Communist movement: Stalin's executions, the persecution of Christians in Russia and China, the discrimination against Jews, the rape of Hungary, the occupation of Czechoslovakia, and the suppression of free speech. This ruthlessness is more than the excess of a young revolution. It is the direct outgrowth of an atheistic doctrine that deifies the system and dehumanizes man.

A close link has been forged in our day between sexual rebellion and political subversion. There is something demonic about the obsession with the obscene. The sick sex now on the scene is a symptom of spiritual rebellion, of man's attempt to tear down his relationship with his Maker. *Time* recently noted that four-letter words have become a tool of protest against the establishment. In the play *Marat-Sade*, the Marquis de Sade says, "The revolution of the flesh will make all your other revolutions seem like prison mutinies." Don Juan may have displaced Prometheus as the figure who embodies rebellion against God. The *Playboy* philosophy of sex as recreation is very much with us; but a greater danger has arisen in unbridled sex as an expression of revolution.

Sex is a direct reflection of man's relation to God, for man was created "male and female" in the "image of God." Man's longing to know a woman is the analogy of man's longing to know God. God demands that a man be faithful to his one wife because otherwise he would destroy his capacity to have a good relationship with the one God. The danger in sexual promiscuity is that it twists the capacity for spiritual fidelity. This is why we should recognize the current campaigns to make adultery and homosexuality respectable for what they really are: rebellious attempts of sinful man to tear down his relation to God.

The abuse of drugs is another part of the anarchist rebellion. Herbert Marcuse, the guru of the New Left, has called for a fight to legalize marijuana as "a means of total opposition." The goal of the protesters has been expressed by the Living Theatre, an American drama group working in Europe, "We want to smash the steel structure of laws which civilization has erected to protect itself from barbarism."

The connection between sexual and political anarchy in the underground newspapers is more than accidental. If we ignore this connection and go around patting all the radical revolutionaries on the head as God's secret agents, then we are spiritually blind, theologically naïve, and politically stupid.

There are some very deep and tragic questions that make it hard for Christians to know how to respond to particular revolutions. An issue that has been debated a great deal recently is whether a Christian should ever take part in violent revolution. A World Council of Churches' consultation on racism concluded, "That all else failing, the church and churches support resistance movements, including revolutions, which are aimed at the elimination of political and economic tyranny which makes racism possible" Many of us, while noting the qualifying phrase, "all else failing," have grave doubts about making the Christian church a sponsor of violent revolution in the sense that seems implied here. Yet this is a difficult question that cannot be answered simply.

Is violent revolution always wrong? This question always provokes near-violent discussion. Each side has its historical precedents. Those who say, "No, it's not always wrong," remind patriotic Americans of the events surrounding 1776. They argue that John Knox held that tyrannicide—the killing of an unjust despot—was sometimes right. They find a model in Dietrich Bonhoeffer, the German pastor and theologian, who joined in the resistance effort to assassinate Hitler. Those who say, "Yes, violent revolution is wrong," argue that history teaches us the demonic aspect of force. The leaders of the French Revolution overthrew the French monarchy violently, but the guillotine caught up with them, too, and Napoleon's dictatorship replaced the monarchy. Communism in Russia substituted its own terror and liquidations for the tyranny of the czars.

So the debate rolls on. But several points can be clearly made. The first is it is never right for the Church to take up the sword in order to promote the Cross. It may have been Mohammad's path to win converts by the sword; it is not Christ's way. When Jesus was arrested Peter drew his sword to defend Him, but Jesus rebuked him, saying, "Put back your sword into its place; for all who take the sword will perish by the sword" (Matthew 26:52). To urge that we "kill a Commie" or "kill a Fascist" for Christ is utter blasphemy.

A second clear teaching of Scripture is that governments have a legitimate right in God's sight to use force in order to restrain evil and lawlessness. Paul wrote to the Roman Christians, living under Caesar's rule, that the ruler "is God's servant for your good. But if you do wrong, be afraid, for he does not bear the sword in vain; he is the servant of God to execute his wrath on the wrongdoer" (Romans 13:4). And what if the ruler overreaches himself, tries to take God's place, and to make men do what is clearly against God's will? Then the believer takes his cue from the first Christians and says, "We must obey God rather than men" (Acts 5:29). It is clear that he resists unjust commands; it is *not* clear that he resists them by violence.

Jesus Christ taught that His followers were to suffer violence done against their persons without resisting. "Do not resist one who is evil. But if any one strikes you on the right cheek, turn to him the other also," He ordered (Matthew 5:39). When He went to His death He embodied His own teaching, for as Peter recalled, "When he was reviled, he did not revile in return; when he suffered, he did not threaten" (1 Peter 2:23).

On this point Christians agree. But hard questions still remain. The Christian may not resist personal aggression against himself. But is it permissible for him to use force or violence to resist those who oppress and kill his family? innocent women and children? entire races or societies? Is there such a thing as a "just" war in the sense that resistance is a lesser evil than the continuation of an abominable evil, such as Hitler's regime? If there are such tragic or justifiable wars, may revolutions be such? And may individual Christians participate in them?

My conviction is that violent revolution is not an option for Christians in countries such as the United States, where there are other ways to change things. One may try to understand how those who have undergone a pattern of constant physical or psychological harassment, because of their color or religion or other factors, may be tempted to lash out in rage. But to understand is not to condone. Especially for the Christian there are other paths to tread.

In *A Genuinely Human Existence*, Bishop Stephen Neill maintains that Jesus

is a revolutionary. Any attempt by either church or state to take his teaching seriously has always had most revolutionary consequences. But it is important to note the method that he follows and the kind of revolution that he is concerned to introduce. He never incites his followers to mass disobedience to the local authorities. He starts no campaign of defiance of the existing order. He will not countenance any kind of violence, knowing well that violence always leads to more violence and that high ideals can easily disappear in the stress of conflict. His method of revolution is both more subtle and more effective than that followed by most of the revolutionaries of this world.

The resort to violence may indicate a failure of moral imagination as well as of spiritual faith. There are other ways in which constructive protest can express itself and a survey of Jesus and His followers suggests some of them:

1. Patient suffering of ill-treatment. Peter held this out as a Christian ideal with Jesus as the model. "If when you do right and suffer for it you take it patiently, you have God's approval. For to this you have been called because Christ also suffered for you, leaving you an example, that you should follow in his steps. . . . When he was reviled, he did not revile in return; when he suffered, he did not threaten; but he trusted to him who judges justly" (I Pet. 2:20 ff.). Patient suffering of this sort does not mean acquiescence in evil; it does mean trusting our case to God until the opportunity comes to take action.

2. Attempts to change the mind and attitude of others. Jesus and His followers did this by example, by teaching and preaching and by prayer. Very seldom today are we reminded of Jesus' command to "pray for those who persecute you." Christians have weapons more powerful than guns—the Word of God and prayer —to change men's minds. When Peter was arrested, "earnest prayer for him was made to God by the church," and God opened iron gates to let him out of prison (Acts 12:1 ff.)! If we set out to persuade others to change, however, we need great patience and tact. How can we help others to abandon prejudice, for example, if we treat them with prejudice and lack of respect?

3. Appeal to the law. On one occasion when Paul was about to be flogged on order of a Roman tribune, he said to the centurion, "Is it lawful for you to scourge a Roman citizen and uncondemned?" When the authorities ascertained his citizenship status they immediately called off the flogging (Acts 22:22 ff.). On another occasion Paul appealed to Caesar's higher court for trial and his case was remanded (Acts 25:11 f.). "Render to Caesar the things that belong to Caesar," said Jesus, and this includes the right to appeal to government for justice. Today when we the people are Caesar in a sense we have even greater oppor-

tunity and responsibility to seek justice through law. Efforts to change and improve law and justice are often disappointing yet they are worthwhile. Law may not make men good; but it may restrain them from evil.

4. Nonconformity to unjust commands. There is a higher authority than kings, party secretaries or presidents. God alone is Lord of the conscience. When the authorities told the first Christians not to preach any more in the name of Jesus, as already noted they appealed to the most supreme court: "We must obey God rather than men." There are occasions when civil disobedience is not only permissible but imperative—when the laws of men contradict the explicit commands of God's Word.

5. The last resort is not violence, but martyrdom. Even "courteous rebels" may be crucified. Some of the high moments of Christian history have come in the martyrdom of men of God, whose blood has been the seed of great good.

Having said all this, let's be fair enough to recognize that it's easy for us in a stable society to give pat answers to revolution, but it's not so easy for our brothers in the Third World or even in the ghettos. A certain humility and sense of history ought to restrain the judgments we pass on other brethren in other situations. An interesting comment was made by an Indonesian Christian who passed through the recent revolution in his own country. "I think the Christians must be in the revolution as people who, while having an open eye for the pretensions of the revolution, at the same time take the promises and the hope of the revolution more seriously than anyone else, infusing a greater sense of realism and responsibility into the thinking of the revolution."

We forget so easily when we are comfortable. At a Fourth of July picnic in a small mid-American town someone passed around a copy of the Declaration of Independence, drawn up as a petition, and asked people to sign it. A number refused because they said it sounded to them like a piece of Communist propaganda!

Revolution is a brew of promise and hope, of evil and rebellion, and of ambiguity. This means that the Christian's role is to give neither blanket condemnation nor blanket approval to the revolutions of the 20th century. Sometimes we may be led to reject change and sometimes to accept it. We may disagree with our

Christian brothers on when to reject and when to accept. But we must refuse to let ourselves be swept along by the tides. Always we must judge what is happening in the light of that greater movement to which we must give priority: the Christian revolution! There is really only one course open to us: to be neither total resisters nor total rebels, but to be revolutionaries—Christian style!

3 REBELS WITH A CAUSE

The year I was born the Korean War ended.

When I was one, the Supreme Court banned racial segregation in the schools.

When I was two, Dr. Jonas Salk's polio vaccine was pronounced a success.

When I was three, America exploded an H-Bomb, the equivalent of 10 million tons of TNT.

When I was four, the Russians launched Sputnik I.

When I was five, Cardinal Angelo Giuseppe Roncalli became Pope John XXIII.

When I was six, Fidel Castro assumed power in Cuba.

When I was seven, John F. Kennedy was elected President.

When I was eight, the Peace Corps was established.

When I was nine, John Glenn orbited the earth.

When I was ten, John F. Kennedy was shot down in Dallas.

When I was eleven, the U.S. Senate passed the Gulf of Tonkin Resolution and North Vietnam was bombed.

When I was twelve, there was a march in a place called Selma.

When I was thirteen, Red Guards appeared in China.

When I was fourteen, Newark exploded and Detroit went up in flames.

When I was fifteen, Martin Luther King, Jr., was slain in Memphis and Robert F. Kennedy in Los Angeles.

When I was sixteen, Neil Armstrong took one small step and made a giant leap for mankind.

I am the NOW GENERATION. These are the events that have shaped my life.   Source unknown.

When we stop to review the march of events a new perspective emerges for us on the youthquake that is shaking our world, this generation that is such a puzzling mixture of long hair and heart-warming honesty, of drug drop-outs and inner-city tutoring programs, of idealism and cynicism, of sit-ins and suicides, of casual openness to sex and protests against pollution, of fascination with Jesus and disinterest in His church.

The over-30s have tended to react in three general ways to the now generation. Some have tried to ignore them, dismissing them with a flip, "It was that way in my day, too." And, of course, youthful rebels are not something entirely new under the sun. We are not the first to gaze in wide-eyed wonder at their actions. Listen to this complaint about the young: "We live in a decadent age. Young people no longer respect their parents. They are rude and impatient. They inhabit taverns and have no self-control." That may sound like the 1970s but actually it is from an inscription found on a 6000-year old Egyptian tomb! Lewis Feuer's *The Conflict of Generations* lists worldwide examples of student activism beginning in the Middle Ages. And Professor Seymour Lipset in a letter to his friends cites some American examples:

Police had to be called to Harvard several times to quell violent rioting between 1807 and 1830. In 1823 half the senior class was expelled. Half of Princeton's students were expelled in 1806 following a rebellion, one of six which occurred in that era. Students occupied college buildings while "Nassau Hall resounded to the reports of pistols and the crash of bricks against doors, walls and windows." Yale and Virginia experienced violent protests against examinations, bad food, politics, morals and religion, "compulsory military training, stupid courses." Back in 1922 philosopher George Santayana threw up his hands at students who "all proclaim their disgust with the present state of things in America; they denounce the Constitution of the United States, the churches, the colleges, the press . . . they are against everything—but what are they for? I have not been able to discover." (Quoted by Ernest van den Haag in *The Atlantic*)

Other adults worship youth in a way that reveals their own frustrations and fears. This is, as one thoughtful observer noted, the first generation in history in which the older generation imitates the kids! Youth has become an obsession. Styles in clothing and language start with the young and go up. Next to "new" and "now" there is no more powerful word in advertising language than the word "young." We are exhorted to Go Young,

Think Young, Live Young, Smoke Young. When asked his formula for success, a British newspaper publisher whose paper had a circulation of five and a half million readers replied, "Very simple. Just ignore the reader over thirty." He went on to explain that readers under thirty are seldom interested in the affairs of those older, but that readers over thirty are very much interested in what the young are doing.

A third reaction is resentment, fear, and even hatred. The very sight of a young face, especially framed by long hair, is enough to make some people absolutely explode in rage against "those blasted kids." "I am tired of the tryanny of spoiled brats," lashes out a college professor in a national magazine.

Youth needs neither to be patronized, petted nor pilloried. What they do need is older people—especially those in the 30–35 age bracket, the "bridge" generation—who will try to listen, to understand, and who have something real to share in terms of authentic experience, and especially genuine experience of God. I second the opinion of Ruth (Mrs. Billy) Graham that "our teenagers are the most intelligent, most gifted, most informed crop of young people that the United States and perhaps the world has ever seen." I agree wholeheartedly with Methodist Bishop Earl Hunt who identifies himself as "a partisan without apology for this generation of young people. They have not turned off Jesus, the church or religion," he claims, "but our abuse of Jesus, the church and religion. Their concerns are religious concerns when you analyze them. They are characterized by idealism and devastating honesty. There has never, in my opinion, been a generation more ripe for conversion to Jesus Christ."

Why then the restlessness and rebellion? Many causes might be cited:

—Natural adolescent rebellion. Youth has a built-in tendency to question and rebel; the succession of generations is a God-given instrument of change. As the old saying goes, "If a young man is not a rebel when he's 17, there's something wrong with his heart; if he's still a rebel twenty years later, there's something wrong with his head." The natural thing is for the youth to find himself by asserting his independence toward father or mother. But when there is no parental authority in the home, no sure set of values, there is nothing to push against! There is no character growth in pushing against a cream puff! So he rebels against everything. King David had a rebellious son, Adonijah, of whom it's recorded, "His father had never at any time displeased him by asking, 'Why have you done thus and so?'" (I Kings 1:6). So today overpermissiveness has generated "rebels without a cause."

—The pressures of an exploding world. Knowledge is doubling every ten years and the demands on students are four times as great as they were on their teachers. Young people are like goldfish, tossed from the security of a tiny bowl into the frightening immensity of a vast ocean.

—Lack of leadership. This has been called the age of the "anti-hero." Youths identify with models more than rules, and there are few charismatic leaders to follow. A *Parade* magazine poll showed that 53.1% of American youth said there was no living person with whom they identified or whom they tried to emulate.

—Prolonged adolescence. Many more years are spent in school. Getting a job, finding out about "real" life, and being responsible for a family are postponed. Many young people feel keenly that they want to "change the world" while still dependent on a check from home. Not being part of the decision-making process makes for frustration.

—Irrelevance is one of the cardinal evils for today's youth. Many feel that their experiences in both church and school have been isolated from the core issues of life.

—Hypocrisy. Phoniness ranks with irrelevance among youth as Public Sin Number One. They rightly question a society that panics at evidence of sexual looseness among the young yet raises no objection to the exploitation of sex in advertising. They wonder about the truthfulness of a country that preaches high democratic ideals yet fails to practice them for all men. They query the sincerity of going around the world to fight a war for freedom while trying to keep a minority "in its place" at home. For many young people hypocrisy has been highlighted by the drug issue. Why should a young person who comes home to a house littered with cocktail glasses, pill bottles, and ashtrays full of cigarette butts listen when his parents lecture him about drugs? But young people have their own version of phoniness: witness those who mount the barricades to rant against a "materialistic" society and wear buttons that say "Make love, not war," yet despise the parents from whom they get their weekly check!

—Loneliness. Even in the middle of a family there can be no communication. The Beatles sang about a girl who left home "after livin' alone for so many years." Loneliness has led many students to drugs or suicide. A student on a huge university campus could be there for four years without ever talking to an adult who will listen and try to understand.

—Fear of the future. One teenager, asked why he used drugs said, "We know that the wrong finger on the right trigger could end the world, so we live for today because tomorrow may never come." Hope is in short supply.

—Social problems. War, poverty, racism, and pollution are real issues. Injustices have stood unquestioned and unresisted for too many generations and young people today are determined to do something about them.

—"Instantism." Allied closely to the above is the insistence of the young that solutions must be found *now* for every problem. Instant communication has produced expectations of instant answers. There is little sense of history, the realization that many of these problems have roots that go far back and cannot be changed overnight.

—Agitation. Professional revolutionaries, whether Communist or radical, sense the political and public relations leverage of youthful protest and take advantage of their just grievances for ulterior motives.

—Emptiness. Former U.S. Ambassador to France Sargent Shriver invited Billy Graham to meet with Paris student leaders, including some radicals and revolutionaries. One of them said, "We are rebelling against soulless materialism." Brought up in affluent society, never having known the privation of Depression days, upper middle class youth especially have had the leisure to learn that "a man's life does not consist in the abundance of things which he possesses." Notes Dr. Robert Gould, director of adolescent psychiatry at Bellevue Hospital, "They see spiritual emptiness, the

loneliness in the home, the lack of communication, the plain un-
happiness, covered up by material possessions and frantic running
around, and they reject it totally." Then too, science has provided
the answers to the questions that start with "how," but not to
those that start with "why."

—Boredom. No "why" results in no goal, and life goes dead.
Rioters at a music festival told reporters, "We have nothing to
live for." Canadian broadcaster Gordon Sinclair, an avowed agnostic and opponent of religion, said, "I disagree with Billy Graham
on almost everything, but one thing I do agree on is that the trouble
with our young people is that they have nothing to live for." Those
who experience with Solomon the "vanity" of life, yet who do not
learn as Solomon said to "Remember now your creator in the days
of your youth," can be expected to lash out. "I want to destroy,"
wrote a student. If the nihilist is right and there is no meaning,
then why not senseless violence to wipe out the vain efforts of
civilization to pretend there is meaning? Why not destroy the lie?

—Plain rebelliousness. Abbie Hoffman, one of the Chicago
Seven, wrote *Revolution for the Hell of It*. Hell indeed backs
much rebellion! David Wilkerson, founder of the Teen Challenge
work with drug addicts, has confessed to a change of mind. Once
he put most of the blame on adults—home, church, government—
for youths in trouble. But now he is convinced that a large proportion of these youths must be held responsible for their own
deeds. They have deliberately chosen to be rebels against God and
man. "An evil man seeks only rebellion," warns the writer of
Proverbs (17:11). For too long we have romanticized all the restless
rebels. The Bible indicates that the troubles of the universe began
with Lucifer's rebellion in heaven (Isaiah 14), and that at the end
of time "the lawless one will be revealed" (2 Thessalonians 2:8).
According to 2 Peter 2:10 (Phillips trans.), "contempt for authority" will characterize the state of society before Christ's return.
Former Ambassador George Kennan issues a somber judgment in
Democracy and the Student Left,

One cannot, therefore, on looking at these young people in all the
glory of their defiant rags and hairdos, always just say with tears in
one's eyes: "There goes a tragically wayward youth, striving roman-
tically to document his rebellion against the hypocrisies of the age."

One has sometimes to say and not without indignation: "There goes a perverted and willful and stony-hearted youth by whose destructiveness we are all, in the end, to be damaged and diminished."

This is probably the most overanalyzed generation of youth in history, and lest I fall into the error of suggesting that the "restless ones" can be explained by adding up all of the above factors (or a dozen more), let me hasten to add that what youth is can't be coldly laid out and dissected. Today's youth are suspicious, and with good cause, of the coldly intellectual approach. Reality, they believe, can't simply be listed and memorized; it has to be experienced. If you can't "feel" what makes youth tick, you can't understand.

Two recent "happenings" involving youth may illustrate what's going on. Both made the headlines, both reached their contemporaries, but they were very different. One was a rock festival held in upstate New York in the summer of 1969. The other was a revival meeting on a Kentucky college campus in the spring of 1970.

The Woodstock festival was tabbed by *Time* as "history's largest happening." An estimated 400,000 youth, mostly between the ages of 16 and 30, gathered on Max Yasgur's 600-acre farm in Bethel, New York. Symbolically, it was probably one of the most significant sociological events of our age. There was a great deal of drug use, some nudity, and an obvious sexual permissiveness. Hundreds had bad drug trips. Yet neutral observers testified to a lack of violence, gentleness, and an air of sharing and concern. Some attributed this to the "Make love, not war" attitude; others to the apathy induced by drugs. What they came for was the message of the music, the hard rock that has been described as the "anthem of revolution."

The tragedy is that many of the young people represented at Woodstock have rejected, ignored, or never really heard Jesus Christ and His message of spiritual revolution. At Woodstock, singer Jimi Hendrix said, "The world needs a big bath, a big scrubdown." Christians agree that the world needs to be cleaned up and believe that Christ can provide the detergent!

On a recent television program a group of young people were asked just what the attraction of Marxism was for their generation. One thoughtful teenager replied, "I guess it's because it offers a platform for social change and demands a costly personal commitment on the part of the individual." It's imperative that we get across to the students of the world that the cause of Christ is far more revolutionary and demanding than any other revolutionary movement.

A major hang-up in communicating the Gospel to young people is that most of us Christians seem about as revolutionary as a cold fried egg. We've got to make it clear that commitment to Christ means more than a vote for motherhood, the power of positive thinking, and the status quo. Tom Skinner, former leader of the Harlem Lords Gang, speaking at a Billy Graham Crusade in Madison Square Garden said, "Once I rejected Jesus Christ as a member of the white power structure and as a docile, nonaggressive individual. But now I've learned that Jesus Christ is a gutsy, contemporary revolutionary." If today's young people could see that, if they could get a new view of a Gospel we have undersold and made to seem cheap, tame and dull, they could lead a great spiritual revolution, a Christian "youthquake" that would shake the world!

The revival at Asbury College in Kentucky was in vivid contrast to Woodstock. What began one Tuesday morning as an ordinary chapel service stretched into a week-long marathon meeting. Students, and later faculty and staff, turned the planned formal service into an informal gathering for testimony, witness, confession, and exhortation. Classes and other activities were suspended. Personal relationships were straightened out and an atmosphere of joy permeated the campus. One spokesman described it as a "continuous love-in." Many students who had known only a nominal kind of Christianity testified to discovering a reality in their experience of God. The word spread and soon visitors were arriving from nearby schools. Some came only to observe, others caught the spirit, including some "way-out" types. Invitations poured in for students to travel to other campuses to tell the story and within two weeks more than 60 campuses from coast to coast had shared in the fall-out of the Asbury happening. Some of them experienced very similar revivals.

What took place was more than a glorified emotional bash, for some students at Asbury have formed folk groups to put their experience of Christ across in modern musical idiom, while others have become deeply involved in witness and service projects to drug users and poor families in nearby ghetto areas. They are determined that their spiritual "high" will motivate some very practical Christianity.

The Christian movement has known its most glorious moments when young people have been captivated by the vision of Christ. Artists have depicted the apostles as being old men, but probably not one of them was over 25 when Christ called him. A group of seven young athletes at Cambridge University were influenced by Dwight L. Moody for Christ and became the forerunners of a student movement at the beginning of this century that sought "the evangelization of the world in this generation." Billy Graham began his phenomenal evangelistic career while still in his 20s. To be sure, our Christian concern must extend beyond the young. If there are more people under 25 than ever before, there are also more over 60 than ever before, as life expectancy increases. The modern obsession with youth must not rob us of compassion for age. But it's still true that the Christian cause cannot win a world without winning its young.

In two years the average age in America will be 24. The task of confronting this changing era with a changeless Christ belongs largely to Christian youth. Theirs is far from the silent generation; so those of us over 30 must urge them not to be silent about Christ. The church has for too long patronized its young people. We have done things for them. We have sponsored evangelistic campaigns and drives on their behalf. Such a pattern will no longer do.

The summer I was 14 as a boy in Canada I underwent a profound spiritual experience. From the time I was a young lad I had known Christ as my Savior. But that year at a summer conference I met a group of young people whose faith was more vibrantly vital than mine. I discovered the possibility of personal communication with God in a new sense. Bible reading and prayer came alive for me. At this very time our family was going through a period of real stress and I felt very lonely and uncertain. But God was using all these events to forge my character and my future. That fall a chapter of the new Youth for Christ organization was formed in my hometown in Canada. Shortly before my 15th birthday I was entrusted with the responsibility of its presidency.

Through monthly rallies and other activities we sought to reach out and share our faith with other young people in our community. It was through this spiritual responsibility entrusted to me in spite of my youth that I first learned to share my faith, to pray, to speak, and to organize. My vision for evangelism was shaped at that time as I came in contact with devoted Christian youth leaders. This never would have happened had not a wise older person refused to "despise my youth." Ever since I have sensed the importance of my own children and other young persons having the opportunity to share their faith youth to youth.

Perhaps what many young people need more than anything else is to learn *how to rebel!* The kind of rebellion that leads either to violent destruction or to sullen submission is useless. But there is a kind of constructive rebellion, patterned after Jesus Christ Himself. In *A Genuinely Human Existence,* Stephen Neill beautifully describes Jesus as "the courteous rebel." Bishop Neill's analysis of Jesus is worth careful study. He points out that Jesus lived as a Jew, accepting His situation in history. While He criticized His people, He never separated Himself, humanly speaking, from them. His attitude toward tradition is instructive. He never took the view that tradition was always wrong, any more than habit is always wrong. Some traditions He accepted wholeheartedly, such as the teachings of Moses and the prophets. Some traditions—such as the paying of the temple tax—He tolerated because no deep moral principle was involved. Other traditions Jesus resisted and repudiated. He ran headlong into conflict with many of the Jewish leaders because of their legalism. They had tried to work out moral rules to cover every possible case. Jesus saw that this actually made men into hypocrites, allowed them to pretend to be religious when their hearts were far from God, and led to the crushing of human freedom and even to positive cruelty. As an illustration He cited the case of a man being allowed to refuse duties to his parents on the grounds that he had a higher obligation to God (Mark 7:9-13).

And what was Jesus' method? First, He insisted that what a man was on the inside determined what he was on the outside. Motives mattered more than external conformity. So He rebuked the Pharisees who washed the outside of the cup but left the inside filthy (Matthew 23:25). What matters most, He taught, was not the blow but the anger that motivated it; not the act of adultery but the lust that led to it (Matthew 5:21 f.). It was man's inner being, He argued, his heart which must be cleansed. "What comes out of a man is what defiles a man. For from within, out of the heart of man comes . . . all these evil things" (Mark 7:20–23). Any revolution that touches the surface without changing the center of man must fail, in Jesus' estimate.

Second, Jesus insisted that relationships mattered more than rituals. He scathingly rebuked the religious people who thought that a ritual washing of their hands was all that God cared about. "This people draws near me with their lips, but their heart is far from me," He quoted from Isaiah (Mark 7:16). The same thing applied to human relationships. A key issue in His controversy with the Pharisees was the Sabbath. Jesus observed the Sabbath. But He asked: What is the purpose of the Sabbath? Wasn't it true that God made the Sabbath for man, not man for the Sabbath (Mark 2:27)? And so was it not a perversion of the Sabbath to forbid acts of healing and helping those in need? "Is it lawful on the sabbath to do good or to do harm, to save life or to kill?" He demanded (Mark 3:1–4). A religion that hardened the heart and made rituals more important than people was a religion gone wrong, according to Jesus. So His revolutionary method was to offer men a new birth of freedom, a new relation to God that would bring man into a new relation to man!

There are those young people today who are becoming rebels with a cause who have found in Jesus Christ a greater revolutionary and a better revolution. Here in his own words, is the story of a University of Chicago student who made just this discovery:

When I was a sophomore in college, I told my parents that I would use any way or means—including political assassination—to overthrow the Government. My philosophy of life was the philosophy of the radical militant. I was fed up with the hypocrisy of society, and felt that a dramatic change in the system of Government and the laws of this country was imperative. The motivating forces of my life were fear, hate, bitterness, frustration, contempt.

This student met a group of Christians and was impressed with the quality of love and life and joy they radiated.

I'd always considered myself an agnostic but when a member of the group shared Jesus Christ with me I was struck with the fact there has to be a God and that He loves me unconditionally and accepts me just as I am. I had no love at all and wasn't exactly satisfied with myself. Even though I wanted this new quality of life the attitude of my heart was, "God, if you are real, prove your love to me in four or five weeks or forget it!" He proved Himself. I found what I had been seeking for nineteen and one-half years. Over a period of two years He has slammed down my fears and doubts and taken away the hatred and bitterness of my life, replacing it with His love. I am still a revolutionist but I am now motivated by love and reason—instead of hate and fear. Jesus is real.*

* From *Collegiate Challenge* magazine. Printed by permission. Copyright © Campus Crusade for Christ, Inc., 1969. All rights reserved.

4 REVOLUTION FOR HEAVEN'S SAKE

Charles Malik of Lebanon, the distinguished Christian statesman and former president of the United Nations General Assembly, has said, "The West is afraid of being revolutionary." Is he correct? If so, then we are traitors to our Christian heritage. History's greatest revolution began, not under a red star in Petrograd in 1917, but under the star of Bethlehem 2000 years ago in the cradle where God invaded history.

Men begin revolutions with riots and gunfire. God began His revolution by singling out Mary, a simple, country girl, and by telling her that the Holy Spirit would cause the very Son of God to be born in her! Mary consented, and the revolution began. That's how God always starts His revolutions: by quietly invading ordinary lives that are open to Him.

When Mary felt the new life stirring in her womb, she knew instinctively that a new world was also stirring. She'd gone to visit her cousin Elizabeth, and as she entered the house Elizabeth cried out, "Blessed are you among women, and blessed is the fruit of your womb! Why is this granted me that the mother of my Lord should come to me?" (Luke 1:42–43). Mary replied in those famous words that we have come to know as the Magnificat, "My soul magnifies the Lord, and my spirit rejoices in God my Saviour, for he has regarded the low estate of his handmaiden. For behold, henceforth all generations will call me blessed; for he who is mighty has done great things for me, and holy is his name! (Luke 1:46–49).

The Magnificat has rightly been called the most revolutionary document in history. In a flight of prophetic and poetic inspiration, Mary went on to speak that day of a many-sided, multifaceted change that God would bring to the world through the baby in

33

her womb. This was the beginning of a spiritual revolution: "he has scattered the proud in the imagination of their hearts"; of a social revolution: "he has put down the mighty from their thrones, and exalted those of low degree"; of an economic revolution: "he has filled the hungry with good things and the rich he has sent empty away." In Jesus Christ God began the great reversal. Human categories were turned upside down, and the proud and the humble, the mighty and the weak, the rich and the poor, switched places.

The picture of Jesus as a revolutionary is foreign to most of us. From Sunday School we still retain the mental image of a Jesus who was preoccupied with lambs—"gentle Jesus, meek and mild" —and so He was. Yet Jesus Christ was also the greatest revolutionary who ever lived. He said, "I came to cast fire on the earth." He came preaching about a revolution that he called the Kingdom of God. He gathered around Him twelve men, and through these men He changed history.

The revolutionary program of Jesus Christ began as a spiritual revolution. "He has scattered the proud in the imagination of their hearts." Our greatest need is for an inner revolution that can transform men's hearts. As Winston Churchill noted when he received the Nobel Prize, "We have learned to control everything except man." Can man's egocentric pride be changed? One dark night a member of the Jewish establishment came to see Jesus. This man was a concerned leader of society. Like many political and intellectual leaders of today as well as a host of average men, he wanted to know how to solve the human dilemma. What would Jesus suggest? Before he could actually bring himself to ask his question however, Jesus interrupted with, "Unless a man is born all over again, he cannot see or enter into the kingdom of God." Without a fresh start, Jesus was saying, you can't even grasp the nature of the problem and the kind of revolution we need. This prescription for a new world began with a new birth!

No educated person today can fail to be impressed with the staggering achievements of man. But at the same time no thinking person can look at the world without being depressed by man's failure to solve his deepest problems.

What's wrong with the world when on the same day our newspapers carried front-page stories of man's first flight into space and of the trial of a man in Israel for his part in the murder of six million Jews?

What's wrong with the world when promises are not enough and we must have contracts; when doors are not enough and we need locks; when laws are not enough and we need police to enforce them?

What's wrong with the world when science, which has solved so many problems, seeks at the same time a way to cure cancer and a way to destroy the world?

What's wrong with the world when education has dispelled so much ignorance and raised the literacy rate, yet the worst wars in history have been fought by the most literate nations? Justice Robert Jackson once pointed out, "It is one of the paradoxes of our time that modern society needs to fear . . . only the educated man."

What's wrong with the world when government and labor and business produce an affluent society but cannot cope with the spiraling rates of crime, suicide, drug addiction, and moral breakdown?

Eleanor Roosevelt told of a visit she once had with Marshall Tito of Yugoslavia. She asked the Communist leader if they had yet achieved his idea of Communism in his country. He laughed, she said, and replied in effect, "No, we have no Communism here. They don't have Communism in the Soviet Union. In fact, there will never be Communism any place in the world until you can somehow eradicate selfishness from men."

Moral aspirins and political pills cannot solve our problem. What we need is radical surgery for cancer of the soul. The philosopher may describe our problem as irrational thought. The psychologist may call it emotional behavior. The sociologist may dismiss it as a "cultural lag." But Jesus diagnosed our problem as a sickness of the soul, a spiritual heart disease that the Bible labels sin. The real problems, He said, are those that come from the inside.

This may seem crude and oversimplified. However, Jesus wasn't naïve enough to suggest that if only everybody had some pious little experience all our problems would disappear. Obviously, if everyone in the world were converted to Christ overnight, we'd still face staggering problems. There would still be hungry people to feed, illiterate people to reach, and urban masses to transport.

Conversion of the human spirit is not the detailed answer to all our problems, but it does provide a platform from which we can begin to tackle those problems. For the basic conflict is the greed, pride, and self-centeredness of the human heart.

As a wise man observed long ago, the man who goes out to change the world must be an optimist, but the man who goes out to change the world without some way of changing human nature is an absolute lunatic!

O. Henry once told the story of a country boy who went off to the big city. He fell in with a bad crowd, forgot the ideals he'd been brought up to honor, and ended up a pickpocket. One day on the street he saw a girl he had known back home. In her face he could still see the purity and radiant freshness of youth. Suddenly a sense of revulsion filled him. Disgust with what he had become overcame him. He felt his cheeks flush hot with shame and, leaning up against a lamppost, he said, "I wish I could die."

That, essentially, is what happened to the first Christians. When they met Jesus and saw what He was they faced up to themselves. They felt ashamed and sick of themselves. They wished they could die—and they did die—to their old selves. But they also underwent a resurrection—to a new life in Christ!

Peter and John and Andrew and the others found that a new dimension had invaded their lives in Christ. Eternity had come into time. God had stepped into history in the person of Jesus. "He that has seen me has seen the Father," said Jesus, and they knew that they were seeing the expression of God in human form.

But this spiritual revolution was more than God invading history and living *among* men; it was God invading personality and living *in* men. When Jesus told His disciples He was going to die and leave them they were desolate. How could they go on without the leader they depended on? But Jesus made a fantastic promise, "I will not leave you desolate; I will come to you . . . and I will pray the Father, and He will give you another Counselor, to be with you forever, even the Spirit of truth" (John 14:18, 16-17).

This promise was fulfilled—with power—at Pentecost. One hundred and twenty followers of Jesus gathered in an upper room on their knees. They had good reason to kneel, for these were the men and women who ran when Jesus was arrested, denied Him when He was tried, hid themselves when He was executed, and locked themselves in a room when He was buried. Yet these were the men and women that Jesus was now ordering into an enemy-occupied world to represent Him. No wonder they were praying!

A mysterious power came upon these people—like a sweeping desert wind, like a consuming forest fire—as the Spirit that Jesus promised gripped them like high-voltage power. No longer was God "out there" or "back there" or "up there." He was present, immediate, real! The evidence was in their lives. Men who had been cowards now "proclaimed the Word of God with boldness" (Acts 4:31). Men who had been obsessed with their weakness now "with great power . . . gave their testimony to the resurrection of the Lord Jesus" (Acts 4:33). They became more conscious of the supernatural world, the spiritual warfare between powers of good and evil. As Paul put it, "Our fight is not against any physical enemy; it is against organizations and powers that are spiritual. We are up against the unseen power that controls this dark world, and "spiritual agents from the very headquarters of evil" (Ephesians 6:12, Phillips trans.). But they also knew there was supernatural power on their side. The evil spiritual forces were not able to resist the commands of the apostles who spoke in Jesus' name. These men discovered new spiritual capacities. The spirit of love and self-lessness that had been in Jesus now dwelt in them. New compassion for others sprang up in them. When there was a famine in Jerusalem, Christians far away in Ephesus sent aid. Like Jesus they were enabled to forgive and love their enemies. Stephen, the first martyr, cried out as they stoned him, "Lord, do not hold this sin against them," just as Jesus on the Cross had prayed, "Father, forgive them."

Indeed, a revolution had happened. An old regime had been overthrown in their lives and a new regime had taken over. Christ had overthrown the old forces of sin and evil and had taken over the master control center of their lives.

This sending of the Holy Spirit upon men and women is at the heart of the revolutionary power of Christian faith. These men were not simply trying to imitate Jesus. Rather, Jesus Christ was living in them. Instead of one Jesus Christ walking around Jerusalem there were now—and I say it reverently—one hundred and twenty Jesus Christs there. As Martin Luther described it, they were "little Christs," men in whom Jesus Christ was continuing to live His life. They had undergone a fantastic spiritual transformation that revolutionized every aspect of their lives—the moral, the social, the economic. Jesus Christ touched them with His power and they, in turn, touched their world with power. They became revolutionaries, Christian style. They touched hypocrisy and turned it into reality. They touched immorality and turned it into purity. They touched slavery and turned it into liberty. They touched cruelty and turned it into charity. They touched snobbery and turned it into equality.

One of the best definitions I ever heard of revolution goes like this, "To take an existing situation which has proved to be unworkable, archaic, impractical, out of date, and to destroy that situation, tear it down and replace it with a system that works."

Now, according to the Bible's diagnosis, there is something unworkable, archaic, and impractical about human nature. It will not work. It cannot do what God wants.

Sin ought to be spelled s–I–n, "the big I." This is what lies at the root of our problems. So Jesus came to earth to take upon Himself this ego-centered, independent, God-denying nature that man has. On the Cross He died bearing in Himself this sin. And He came to replace our nature, which will not work with His nature, one that will!

To today's world longing for positive revolution, Jesus Christ offers a strategy for change that really works. First, we must *be convinced* of the reality of the God apart from whom no change is possible. He is the author of human history, the ground of human worth. Apart from Him life is a meaningless gamble, and any effort to change things for the better is absurd! Second, we must *be changed.* The Christian recipe for changing the world involves changing men. Each man must face the fact that he is part of the world's problem, recognize the sin and self-centeredness in his own life, receive the power of the Living Christ who died to make us whole, and reorient his life toward the future under God's control. It's hypocritical nonsense to talk about changing the world when we are unwilling to let God change us. Third, we need to *be together.* A log on the fireplace by itself will soon go out, but placed with others it keeps glowing. So an essential part of Jesus' strategy is to bring His people together in a renewing fellowship. Fourth, we must *be moving* in action for Christ. Changed men, not in isolation, but involved in the real world can make a genuine difference.

Our world is going to have a revolution. Have no doubt about it. The question is which revolution: the revolution of hate and violence or Christ's revolution of love and spiritual power?

The same choice arose in Jesus' day. During His lifetime there was injustice. The Jewish people were being exploited by the Romans who occupied their country. A Roman soldier could walk up to a Jew and say, "Carry my bag for a mile," and the Jew had no avenue of protest.

In the countryside and the hills of Judea there arose bands of guerrilla revolutionaries. Like the militant revolutionaries of today, they began to preach revolutionary doctrine to the people. "There is only one way to deal with these Roman pigs. Burn them out! Kill them!" There were riots, demonstrations, and protests. There were a few abortive attempts to overthrow the government. There was bloodshed and violence.

It was just at that time that Jesus Christ came with another revolution. He had no sword. He came preaching about the Kingdom of God. He came demonstrating love. He came to walk side by side with the sinners and the ordinary people of His day. He gave them a glimpse of another kind of world.

To the militants of His day Jesus would have said, "You are right. Society is corrupt. It's no good. But after you get through burning everything down what are you going to replace the system with? I have come to create a whole new system. If you will open yourself to me I will put my life into you. And you will walk around as a respresentative of the Kingdom of God here on earth, with God Himself living in you."

The time came when Barabbas was caught and arrested. So was Jesus. And Pilate, the Roman Governor, found himself with two revolutionaries on his hands. At the Passover time he brought them out to the crowd and said, "It's a custom to release one prisoner to you at the time of the festival. Now who do you want me to release—Barabbas or Jesus?" And the people answered, "Give us

Barabbas." Then Pilate said, "What shall I then do with Jesus which is called Christ?" And they all said, "Let him be crucified."

Nineteen long centuries have passed. But basically the issue remains the same. Which revolutionary shall we choose—Barabbas or Jesus Christ?

5   LOVE IN A LOPSIDED WORLD

Some months ago our family took a vacation in the beautiful mountains of western North Carolina. One night we decided to play a game of Monopoly. Early in the game my wife took posession of Park Place and Boardwalk. Those who have played the game will remember that these are expensive properties and if you land on them you have to play fantastically high rents. My wife kept putting houses and hotels on them and bought a whole section of new properties; the rents kept skyrocketing. Soon it became clear what was happening. The rest of us just didn't have the capital to keep up, no matter how hard we tried. One after the other we left the game, mortgaged to the hilt, and finally bankrupt.

It was just a game and it was all in good fun. But as we sat in comfort enjoying a perfect summer evening, my mind turned to the rest of the world. That game of Monopoly, it seemed to me, was a picture of what was happening in the world: the rich getting richer and the poor getting poorer. Only in reality it is a game in which the stakes are life or death.

It is almost impossible for us in rich, comfortable, overstuffed North America to realize that the greatest disaster in history may be just around the corner, as the population outraces the food supply.

The world is close to mass starvation. In *Famine–1975!* W. and P. Paddock predict that "by 1975 a disaster of unpredecented magnitude will face the world. Famines, greater than any in history, will ravage the undeveloped nations!" Paul Ehrlich, author of the best-selling *The Biological Bomb*, issues a similar gloomy warning that "there is not the slightest hope of escaping a disastrous time of famines from 1975 onward. It is shockingly apparent that the battle to feed man will end in a rout." Long before Ehrlich Jesus predicted that until the end of time there would be famines in various places (Luke 2:10). We cannot realistically expect to end hunger once and for all. But that does not free us from Christian responsibility and concern to do all we can now!

We saw how Jesus' revolution began with a spiritual transformation in individual lives. But it did not end there. Christ's revolution brought a change in every aspect of his followers' lives—economic, social, and moral. The Book of Acts gives us a series of glimpses of the early Christians scattered in the cities of the Roman Empire, a band of revolutionaries, Christian style.

At Jerusalem we see an economic revolution. "All who believed were together and had all things in common; and they sold their possessions and goods and distributed them to all, as any had need" (Acts 2:44–45). They had all things in common, but they were not "Communists." Christ's love, not men's demands, led them to share. Later Acts records that "the company of those who believed were of one heart and soul, and no one said that any of the things which he possessed was his own, but they had everything in common" (Acts 4:32). As a result, "with great power the apostles gave their testimony to the resurrection of the Lord Jesus" (Acts 4:33). The ring of truth was in their words because people saw the self-sacrifice of Jesus in their deeds!

The Holy Spirit, the cutting edge of redemption, was working out *in* them what Jesus had taught *to* them. Jesus had said that the Spirit of the Lord God had anointed Him to "preach good news to the poor" (Luke 4:18). He had fed the hungry; he had warned against the danger of riches. He had told the rich young man seeking life to sell what he had and give to the poor (although He did not demand that of every rich man). He had said, "How hard it is for a rich man to enter into the kingdom of God." About one-fifth of all that Jesus taught concerned the use of money and possessions.

Don't you think Jesus would have something to say about this coming famine? Don't you think He would have something to say to the rich nations about the poor nations? We have soft-pedalled this revolutionary implication of Christian faith for too long. If the Christian revolution isn't big enough to make a difference in the area of our economic responsibility, then it isn't big enough. According to the Bible, the salvation of the spiritual must be worked out in the stewardship of the material. As 1 John 3:17 asks, "If anyone has the world's goods and sees his brother in need, yet closes his heart against him, how does God's love abide in him?"

Sometimes I think that the problem is so big that it's hard to see "our brother's need." If a starving baby lived next door we would see it and probably do something. But how can we visualize millions of babies with wrinkled stomachs in India, in Vietnam, or in the Sudan? Let me draw a picture for you that may help you as it has helped me.

Suppose all the world could be compressed into a town of 1000 people. In this town 330 would be rich while 670 would be poor. Sixty-nine of the 1000 would be North Americans. These 69 would have one-half of the total income, one-seventh the food, and one-half the telephones. The rich would have ten times as many doctors as the poor, fifteen times as many nurses, twelve times as many hospital beds, twenty-five times as many newspapers, ten times as many radios, and five times as many books. This is indeed in Barbara Ward the British economist's apt phrase a "lopsided world." And as she has pointed out further, every year the affluent world *adds* to its wealth more than the entire income of the poor world!

Will God not hold us responsible for our wealth? He sent Amos, the prophet, to announce judgment to the people of Israel because they "trampled upon the needy, and brought the poor of the land to an end."

Writing in *His* magazine, Francis Breisch raises the hard question, "Do we believe in the God of Amos? Is He rebuking us for the materialism that measures good by GNP, Dow-Jones averages, and high priced homes? Is He challenging the hedonism that focuses our attention on second summer vacations, toothpaste with sex appeal, Playboy bunnies and accessory-laden automobiles?"

A survey showed that the two most frequently asked questions in America are: "How can I lose weight," and "Where can I park my car?" How must that sound in the ears of a God who also hears the cry of starving babies in Bombay and Biafra? An Asian visiting America said that his most vivid impression was the size of our garbage cans.

Is all this to say that we ought to feel a sense of guilt for our wealth? Not at all. What we ought to feel is a sense of gratitude and responsibility. Deuteronomy 8:17–18 warns, "Beware lest you say in your heart, 'My power and the might of my hand have gotten me this wealth.' You shall remember the Lord your God, for it is He who gives you power to get wealth." We are not God's special pets; we are His stewards. He has given us our wealth to use for God and for the sake of other men.

Our temptation is to become fat and sleek, selfish and complacent. A revolution is needed in our thinking about money and possessions. Even we Christians get sucked into consuming more and more as material things become our God. The horsepower under the hoods of our cars and the square inches on our color television screens become more important than the call of God. We need a spiritual revolution that will affect our checkbooks as much as our hymnbooks! We need to see that when Jesus Christ revolutionizes a man's life, He revolutionizes his attitude toward his possessions.

In Jesus' story of the Good Samaritan He illustrated three perspectives on life. There were the thieves who robbed the traveler on the lonely, thug-infested road to Jericho. Like those who deliberately exploit the poor, their attitude was, "What's yours is mine. I'll take it." There were the priests and the Levites who passed by, refusing to get involved with a bleeding man in a ditch. Like those today who are so busy (going to a prayer meeting? or running an evangelistic service?) that they just ignore the poor, their attitude was, "What's mine is mine. I'll keep it." And then there was the Good Samaritan who stopped, looked, and acted; who picked up the wounded man and ministered to him; who took him to the inn and paid the bills and promised to come back and take a continuing interest. His attitude was, "What's mine is God's. I'll share it."

We need to recover this revolutionary principle of seeing everything we own as a common trust, committed to us by God, to be used for the common good.

It is not absolutely necessary that we follow the early Christians' pattern of communal living. Apparently this was a fairly short-lived experience, as has been true of most communes. In our own day many young people, not only the hippies, have been attracted to the idea of a simple community where the attitude is one for all and all for one.

The *National Observer* recently reported in depth on one such experiment in a valley in eastern Washington. At the beginning of the commune's existence everyone lived in one big, old house, sharing everything. But soon the house became filthy and infested with flies. The hard workers moved out and built their own cabins and left the lazy ones on their own. At last someone set the house on fire to drive out the transients. One girl comments on the experience:

True communal life just didn't work out. Everyone contributed according to his ability, alright, but those who had less ability seemed to have more needs. I think if everyone had shared the same respect for the amount of time it takes to produce something, whether it is chopping firewood or baking bread, it would have worked. But it got pretty discouraging when you would chop firewood all day to keep the house warm and someone would leave the door open for a couple of hours. I would bake a loaf of bread for dinner and someone would eat it for a snack.

True, some communes have had a much better experience than this. But the experience of the communes, while containing some important lessons, has a limited relevance to the millions of Christians who continue to live in the mainstream of life. What we need is not so much to take the communal pattern of the early Christians as an absolute model. We need to take their principle and apply it to our daily lives: "What's mine is God's. I will share it."

Those early Christians had learned this lesson. They did not ask, "Am I my brother's keeper?" They knew that because of Jesus Christ they were their brother's brother! The problems of one were the concern of all. If there was a famine in Jerusalem it was the concern of Christians far away in Corinth or Ephesus, just as today a famine in Hong Kong should matter to Christians in New Jersey suburbs and Iowa prairies.

If we believe that the earth is the Lord's and the fullness thereof, if we believe that the Lord Jesus Christ became poor that we might become rich eternally through His death for us on the Cross, if we truly believe that as Christians we really own nothing, but are merely administrators of a part of God's estate, then how can we help being part of Christ's economic revolution in a world that staggers along half-stuffed and half-starved?

We can make our influence felt as citizens in helping to order the priorities of society. The United States, Great Britain, Canada, and France spend some $50 billion each year on alcohol and tobacco? Suppose a ten-cent tax were put on every dollar spent for alcohol and tobacco. That would nearly double the entire foreign aid program of these countries. This is not to suggest that an oversimplified mammoth giveaway program dumping millions or billions of dollars would solve all the problems of underdeveloped countries. The problem is more complicated than that. I am convinced that there must be a basic spiritual and moral foundation for the economic health of any country. But certainly there would be some response if every Christian in North America wrote to his government representative urging that his country aim at setting aside one per cent of the total national income each year for some type of direct help overseas. Each of us can also exercise an influence as individuals. We can give through our church agencies and we can invest our lives.

Larry Graham is a young doctor. He plans to practice medicine in Oklahoma with three other Christian doctors. These men have an understanding that each of them will go overseas for several months every two years as a volunteer in a medical mission while the others cover for him.

Brooks Herman runs one of Florida's largest poultry operations. He was led to help the Latin American Mission set up a hatchery on a mountainside in Costa Rica. Because of his contributions, his extended visits, technical help, and guidance, they are now producing 8000 chicks per week. This poultry project is rapidly increasing the production of needed proteins in a country that has one of the highest population growth rates in the entire world.

Charles Barrows is a retired California rancher. A longtime member of the Gideons organization, when he retired he and his wife took a trip to Southeast Asia to distribute Bibles. While they were visiting Manila an appointment was made for him to present a special gift Bible to President Marcos of the Philippines. The President became interested in his visitor and the five-minute appointment stretched into an hour. When he found that Mr. Barrows was an expert farmer he began to discuss the agricultural problems of the Philippines with him.

Finally at the end of the appointment the President said, "Mr. Barrows, we need an agricultural adviser with your qualifications. Why don't you stay here and work for us for $1 a year?" The Californinan was flabbergasted at first; but he quickly recovered and after a hasty consultation with his wife he agreed.

For three years, a period they look upon as one of the most enjoyable and productive of their lives, the Barrowses have lived in the Philippines, working with farmers, teaching in colleges and schools, helping with construction projects, assisting in the work of various missionaries, and at the same time distributing their Bibles and sharing their Christian faith.

Here are just three examples: a young man beginning his professional life, an established businessman, and a retired farmer, each of who is demonstrating the economic power of Christ's revolution. Someone may say that this is just a drop in the bucket, a tiny scratch on the surface of the world's needs. And so it is. But God has a way of multiplying the individual's contribution as Jesus multiplied the five loaves and two fishes and used them to feed 5000 people. The fact that we cannot do everything does not mean that we should not do something.

Again the revolutionary choice confronts us. Will we be like the fool, described by Jesus in His parable, whose barns would not hold his goods and who planned to pull them down and build bigger ones, only to have the voice of God say to him, "You fool, tonight your soul will be required of you, then who will get all those things you provided for yourself"? Will we be like the rich young man who came to Jesus seeking life but who turned away sadly because he had great riches? Or will we take our part with David Livingstone, that intrepid missionary to the interior of Africa, who said, "I will place no value on anything I may have or possess except as it shall further the Kingdom of God"?

We can help to cause the right kind of revolution. We can help to capture man's mind and heart with the revolution of Jesus Christ. But whether the black flag of anarchy, the hammer and sickle of Communism, the dollar sign of capitalism, or the Cross of Christ speaks to the people of this world will depend in part on our answer to this question.

6 IS MORALITY DEAD?

In the third century B.C. China's first emperor, Ch'in shih Huang Ti, linked up some existing walls to create the Great Wall. This gigantic structure stretched for 1500 miles, defending China against barbarians from the north. Later it was widened until a column of troops could march on top, or chariots ride abreast. China's Great Wall remains one of the world's wonders, and is probably one of the few man-made objects astronauts will be able to pick out from the moon. But for defensive purposes the Wall proved to be a magnificent failure. When China's enemies wanted to breach it they didn't have to knock it down. They simply bribed a gatekeeper.

Modern nations—as their ancient counterparts—spend a fantastic proportion of their budgets on defense. Since World War II the United States alone has spent one trillion (1,000 billion) dollars for destructive weapons. But how ironic if the Pentagon should be to modern America what the Great Wall was to ancient China—a symbol of military strength which proved vain because moral values were for sale to the highest bidder! What can military might avail a nation whose integrity has gone?

Billy Graham believes that "we are in the midst of a major moral revolution that is just as important for the survival of America as the revolution led by George Washington and his compatriots was nearly 200 years ago." And historian Arnold Toynbee's oft-quoted assessment is worth remembering: that nineteen of the world's twenty-two great civilizations have collapsed not from outside pressure but from moral decay within.

Moral deflation is a far greater problem for the free world today than monetary inflation. The moral drain is more critical that the gold drain. Everywhere we can see the bitter fruits of moral carelessness, whether in the flaunting of sex, the glorification of violence, or the disregard for human life on the highways.

Neither pot nor pornography forms the moral crisis of our time. That crisis lies in the widely held assumption that no standard is really important. There have always been those who have violated society's moral codes. But ours is a generation in which millions of youth and adults alike repudiate the idea of any binding authority, even God's on their lives.

The Jewish philosopher, Dr. Will Herberg, has warned that "to violate moral standards while at the same time acknowledging their authority is one thing. To lose all sense of the moral claim, to repudiate all moral authority and every moral standard as such, is something far more serious."

The Generation Gap widens at Morality Canyon. Many young people are rebelling at what they call "phoniness" in adult morals. And they are right! Many of us in the over-thirty generation accept moral contradictions blindly and without protest. Our society has become upset, with good reason, at the alarming rise in the use of drugs. Estimates are that from five to twenty million American youth have tried marijuana. Yet why should a young person who comes home to find a house littered with cocktail glasses, cigarette butts, and pill bottles pay much attention when his parents lecture him about using drugs? Parents get worked up about a Columbia University coed who announced that she was living with her boyfriend, yet the same parents see nothing wrong in advertisers exploiting sex to sell their products.

At the same time the younger generation has its own moral hang-ups. Hippies reject their families but accept checks from home. University students get steamed up about social justice, yet shoplifting and pilfering have become serious problems in many university towns. One coed was arrested while walking out of a college store with a book on ethics hidden under her coat. On the other side of this coin is the transparently sincere desire of many young people not to evade moral imperatives, but to find what they regard as a relevant morality. They want to shift from what they regard as society's "phony" double standards to a genuine moral commitment to the real gut issues of our world.

Baptist theologian Kenneth Chafin has neatly capsuled the different perspectives with which youth and adult look at the moral crisis when he says, "Young people today tend to be ideal-istic about social issues and relativistic about personal morality, while their elders often are just the opposite." The older genera-tion finds signs of moral breakdown in sex relations outside marriage, cheating on examinations and tax returns, the rising crime rate, and in disrespect for the law. The young might be more likely to point to racism, militarism, and the hypocrisy of a society that doesn't practice what it preaches about justice and brotherhood.

An editorial in *Life* magazine has updated the list of seven deadly sins. According to *Life*, Irrelevance, Hypocrisy, Selfishness, In-tolerance, Indifference, Cruelty, and Prudery have ousted the traditional sins of Pride, Covetousness, Lust, Anger, Gluttony, Envy, and Sloth as the worst of sins in the catalogue of the new morality.

The present moral debate illustrates that we are really expe-riencing a crisis in authority. As long as each man is free to pick and choose his own pet vices and virtues and disregard the others we are in grave danger. What we need is to rediscover a moral authority and power that can give us the basis for both personal purity and social concern and equip us to live what we profess.

Recently I talked with a lovely young mother who became a Christian during the Billy Graham Crusade in London, England, as a debutante some years ago. She visited her home not long ago, and was amazed and delighted to find that many of her friends, who a few years ago were amused at spiritual things, have now become Christians. In each case she found that these young parents were alarmed at the moral decay surrounding them and for the first time seriously considered the Christian faith as the only way to find some firm moral standards to pass on to their children.

Several years ago large portions of the Eastern seaboard were plunged into total darkness. Office workers were trapped without light in New York and other large cities. Hospitals had to go on emergency power. An entire grid covering tens of thousands of square miles had been thrown out of action, because a trans-former had blown out in one Canadian power station. A huge slice of modern technological society was crippled. Today we are suffering from a widespread moral power failure, and a great portion of man's life is crippled because of a breakdown in our spiritual transformers!

The current moral crisis demands better laws, more compassionate action for the disadvantaged and the poor, fair law enforcement, and improved psychological treatment. But above all it calls for a recovery of spiritual power.

A couple of generations ago an old judge in the Kentucky hills had what he called his "lunacy test." If someone was brought to him to be judged sane or insane, the judge would give him a ladle and tell him to empty a bucket into which water was running from a tap. If the person turned off the tap first the judge ruled him sane, but if he tried to empty the bucket while the water was still running, the judge knew he was crazy!

If we think we can deal with moral decline without going to the source, without turning off the tap so to speak, then *we* are crazy. As a teenager who had been on drugs said, "There is no answer to drug abuse without going to the source of the problem, and by the source I don't mean where people get their narcotics. It has to do with the heart."

This sequence of spiritual depravity issuing in moral decay is underlined in the Bible. As Paul argues in the first chapter of his letter to the Romans, "When men gave God up and would not even acknowledge Him, God gave *them* up to doing everything their evil minds could think of. Their lives became full of every kind of wickedness and sin" (Romans 1:28–29). He made the same point in writing to the Christians at Ephesus. Unredeemed men, he said, "are blinded and confused . . . they are far away from the life of God because they have shut their minds against Him, and they cannot understand His ways. They don't care anymore about right and wrong and have given themselves over to impure ways" (Ephesians 4:18–19, LNT).

First men get away from God and then their moral vision becomes blurred. There is a pregnant phrase in the Old Testament that speaks of the "God of Abraham, the awe of Isaac." To Abraham God was real in a firsthand way. But Isaac his son was one generation removed from spiritual reality. His was a second hand faith. He still believed in his father's God, but in a hand-me-down sort of fashion. Then in the third generation the moral decay set in. Jacob, Isaac's son and Abraham's grandson, was a man shot through with deceit and moral treachery. He deceived his father, his brother, and his uncle. Then he, too, had an encounter with the Living God one lonely night and underwent a personal and moral transformation. This three-generation cycle is significant, for there are millions who are living in the spiritual momentum of the past. As Clare Boothe once put it, "we have become coupon clippers of the spiritual investments of our forefathers." Thousands of parents have no faith, no living spiritual legacy to pass on. This may account largely for today's moral breakdown, for moral purity is the fruit; spiritual dedication is the root.

Louis Cassels, the United Press religion writer, sized up the moral climate of the seventies in a recent article. A godless universe, he wrote, gives no compelling reason to regard the rights of others. While recognizing that some atheists live highly moral lives, Cassels noted that

the vast majority of human beings find it hard enough to behave decently, justly and generously toward others even when they believe that the moral code is sanctioned by a righteous God. Take away that unbelief or undermine it with sufficient doubt—and there is left, for most people, no inner resource strong enough to withstand the test of any serious temptation.

And he concluded, "Until the idea of God is reborn in the minds and hearts of men, it is probably futile to hope for a renaissance of morals."

Three moral options are on the horizon. One is *total license,* the "anything goes" mentality of the permissive society, which would bring upon us a moral anarchy equivalent to ancient Sodom. In reaction to this there could come *total control.* People in disgust and despair would be willing to turn power over to a dictator who would promise to clean up the mess. The other choice lies in *total commitment* by an overwhelming minority of those who will let God use their lives to help reverse the moral tide.

Could that happen? It has happened before! It could happen again!

Twenty centuries ago there was a little band of Christian revolutionaries. In the middle of a pagan and corrupt society they were "the light of the world" and "the salt of the earth." Probably it was in Corinth that they stood out most clearly in contrast to the surrounding society.

Corinth was a cesspool of evil and perversion. It was a city infamous in the ancient world for its moral muck and slime, a byword for every kind of vice. The Greeks even had a word for it. "To be a Corinthian" meant to live with a candle lit at both ends and to throw away all moral scruples. The city had a reputation for sexual license because it was the center for the worship of the goddess of love. As a seaport it was known for greed, blackmail and cheating, and every kind of sin.

To this city Paul came preaching Christ crucified and many of the Corinthians believed him. He stayed there eighteen months spreading the Word of God among them. Later he wrote a letter to the Christians in that city, cataloguing the vice of Corinth. "Don't fool yourselves. Those who live immoral lives—who are idol-worshippers, adulterers or homosexuals—will have no share in his kingdom, neither will thieves or greedy people, drunkards, slander-mongerers or robbers" (1 Corinthians 6:9–10). Then he exclaims, "And such were some of you. But you were washed, you were sanctified, you were justified in the name of the Lord Jesus Christ and in the Spirit of our God" (1 Corinthians 6:11). The tides of God's grace had swept in and carried the trash off the beach of their lives.

Was it Paul's personality that changed these people? Not at all. It was the power of Jesus Christ. Jesus had given them in Himself and in His teaching a model of what a man ought to be.

During a visit to Tokyo a friend of mine met a young Japanese boy and introduced him to a missionary acquaintance. Some weeks later the boy wrote and gave his impressions of the missionary, "I look in his eyes and see that this is the kind of man who is hard with himself and gentle with others." This is what the early Christians saw supremely in Jesus Christ: self-discipline, His refusal to give in to what was mean and base and impure, and

His one desire to do what pleased God no matter what it cost Him. At the same time they recognized in Him a love and gentleness toward others, even when they had failed. His was the kind of purity that made Him compassionate rather than harsh.

Jesus lived by the rules—a straight-arrow—but He did so in love. He taught that the Ten Commandments are important but that keeping them depends on our motives as well as actions. What matters isn't just the insulting word, or the blow, or the immoral act—but also the angry thought, the hatred, the lustful thought that gives birth to the action. And Jesus summarized all the law in one word: love! Love God and your neighbor as yourself!

But Jesus gave them more than a model. He also gave them a motive for morality.

Several years ago the Air Force Academy in Colorado expelled some cadets for cheating. They had broken the honor code and had been reported by fellow cadets. Here were men who were willing to live by fierce loyalty to an honor code for the sake of leadership. The first-century Christians at Corinth were not changed by a moral code but by a fierce loyalty to Jesus Christ, who had died for them. Their morality sprang not from a cold sense of duty to a far-off ideal but from the glad devotion of hearts that had been made free. They were gripped by the truth that Paul wrote to them, "God has bought you with a great price. So use every part of your body to give glory back to God because He owns it" (1 Corinthians 6:20, LNT).

In addition to a model and a motive Jesus Christ also brought a moral dynamic to men. "Your body is the home of the Holy Spirit," Paul wrote, "and He lives within you" (1 Corinthians 6:19 LNT). What changed these men? The same power that raised Jesus Christ from the dead. Both these miracles—the resurrection and the moral transformation in their lives—were demonstrations of God's power in the midst of human weakness, and here is our moral imperative today. We know we shouldn't lie and steal and lust and be selfish but where do we get the power to lead different lives?

In Newark, New Jersey, I met a high school senior who was reared in Newark's worst ghettos. When he was six his father, an alcoholic, left home. By the time this boy reached fourteen he had been arrested for larceny, breaking and entering, and arson. He was sleeping in burned-out buildings and fighting had become his way of life. Then he was invited to Calvary Church in Newark. There he met a group of young people who knew Christ in a vital and personal way. He found a pastor who was honest with him, and a Lord and Savior in Jesus Christ. He went back to high school to become an all-state basketball player and is now enrolled in a Christian college, hoping some day to preach the Gospel of Christ!

Without a moral revolution can we survive? Edmund Burke wrote many years ago, "Men are qualified for civil liberties in exact proportion to their disposition to put moral chains upon their own appetites. Society cannot exist unless a controlling power on will and appetite be placed somewhere, and the less of it there is within, the more there must be without . . . men of intemperate minds cannot be free. Their passions forge their fetters."

The total license of moral anarchy. The total control of dictatorship. Or the total commitment of the Christian moral revolution. These are the choices—and the hour for decision is upon us.

7 BRIDGE OVER TROUBLED WATERS

On a warm spring Sunday I was the guest preacher in a very beautiful and fashionable church that had impeccable credentials for its orthodox Christianity. The sanctuary was packed. The music was outstanding. The atmosphere was reverent. The people were eager and attentive. I spoke that morning about Jesus' encounter with a social outcast, a scoundrel of a tax collector named Zacchaeus, an encounter that illustrated Jesus' longing to "seek and save those who are lost." Afterward the comments were warm and gratifying.

Later that day, to my dismay, I heard that some Negro people had tried to enter the church for the service and had been refused admission by the ushers. Some weeks before the church had been the target of a racial demonstration. As a result the church officials had decided, as a matter of policy, that Negroes arriving at the church in groups of two or more would automatically be assumed to be demonstrators, not worshipers, and would be denied entrance. And apparently the several Negroes who came that morning had arrived together rather than singly, and the policy had been applied to them.

Some further reports produced the information that one of the black visitors had been a soldier from a nearby military base, due to leave in a few days for Vietnam. Having read in the paper that a Billy Graham Team member would preach at that church on Sunday morning, and knowing of Billy Graham's reputation for preaching to all people, he had set out to find the church, but found the door barred to him.

Anguish would hardly be strong enough to describe what I felt. Here I was, preaching about a Christ who came in love and openness to society's outcasts, and the church that represented that Christ was barred to a black man, who as it turned out, might well confront death shortly. What the man's motives in coming were I do not fully know. Some people later suggested that he had been "prompted" to come by some out-of-state agitators. But whatever his motives, I could not help but think that Zacchaeus' motives were fairly murky. Apparently sheer curiosity led him down to see Jesus passing through Jericho. Nevertheless Jesus welcomed him and went to stay at his house.

We located the name and address of that soldier and I wrote to him, expressing my personal apology, and assuring him of a welcome to any future service in which I might be taking part. I wrote to the pastor of the church (who no doubt found himself pulled from one side by reactionaries and attacked from the other by radicals) and expressed to him my own protest at the policy they had established. I issued a public statement that I would never knowingly speak in a church that had racial bars. And later when a clergyman friend of mine was going to Vietnam I arranged for him to contact the soldier, give him my personal greetings, and witness to him of the love of Christ.

Yet when all this was done, there remained the sobering sense that we Christians have so far to go in obeying the implications of the Gospel of Christ in terms of our love for all men.

If you read the New Testament, you can't help but see how Jesus broke down all the barriers that might have divided man from man. When he chose Simon the Zealot as a disciple He broke down political barriers. By dining with Zacchaeus He ignored class barriers. In talking with a woman of Samaria He put aside social barriers. In heeding the appeal of the Syrophoenician woman and praising the faith of the Roman centurion, He bypassed racial and national barriers. He allowed a woman who was a sinner to touch Him, quietly forgetting the barrier of reputation. A poor widow gave her mite and He held her up for praise, overlooking economic barriers. When the disciples' feet were dirty He washed them, not minding the barrier between master and servant. Yet when the disciples criticized a follower who did not belong to their group He rebuked their intolerance, setting aside denominational barriers. As a baby, an old man rejoiced in Him;

as a young man, children flocked to Him; He crossed the gaps of age. He was a bridge across troubled waters. His love never was stopped by a wall.

When the Christian revolution first began, Jesus Christ not only brought man into a new relationship with God. He also broke down the walls between men. He brought about a social revolution. As Mary put it in the Magnificat, "He has put down the mighty from their thrones and exalted those of low degree."

In the city of Antioch we see this social revolution at work. "In the church at Antioch there were prophets and teachers, Barnabas; Symeon, who was called Niger; Lucius of Cyrene; Manaen, a member of the court of Herod the tetrarch, and Saul" (Acts 13:1). There were two Jews, two Africans, and a Roman aristocrat. All races and classes had become beautiful in Christ.

In sad contrast, it is to the shame of the Christian church that we have been so slow to face the demands of the Gospel in the 20th-century racial revolution. With some notable exceptions we have moved only when we have been run over from behind. Too many white Christians have supposed they enjoyed a privileged position at some "white hand of God."

What does this have to do with the Gospel? Well, let me ask what kind of Gospel we are preaching when a church sends missionaries to convert Africans but suggests to the black man at home that he go to his own church with his own kind? Why should the Negro listen to us talk about a home in Heaven when we refuse to make him at home in our neighborhood and our school? I cannot forget the burden of a friend of mine, ministering in a certain town where age-old prejudices have held fast. He said, "I want to do something to help win Negroes in our town to Christ, but it seems like such a mockery to try to evangelize them when I can't even invite them to come worship in my Church!" What, I ask you, does this not have to do with the Gospel and evangelism?

Our world has been torn apart by racial crisis. Lord Carradon, British Ambassador to the United Nations, said, "I am convinced that race is the most explosive and dangerous issue the world must face." What does the Bible have to say in this crisis?

Basic to the teachings of the Bible is that mankind as God's creation is one, biologically and spiritually. The first chapters of Genesis show all men coming from a single pair. After the flood destroyed the ancient world unity was restored to man through Noah's family. Paul took this idea of man's biological unity to affirm that man also has a spiritual affinity that made it possible for sin to spread to all men. "As sin came into the world through one man and death through sin so death spread to all men because all men sinned" (Romans 5:12). When Paul talked to the philosophers on Mars Hill in Athens, he stressed that God "made from one every nation of men to live on all the face of the earth" (Acts 17:26).

Another clear teaching of the Bible is that all men have a special importance and dignity because they have been created in the image of God" (Genesis 1:26-27). Regardless of a man's race or class or background he is stamped with this image. So James 3:9 warns us not to "curse men who are made in the likeness of God."

In a fascinating interview on British television, Prince Philip commented on a widespread range of subjects. When he was asked about racialism the Prince pointed out that race is not simply a matter of color. "What is distinctive of the Scot or the Welshman but race?" he asked. "There is a lot of tribalism in us still." He went on to point out that a few hundred years ago there was only one book that everybody in the Western world read—the Bible. Today, however, we get our intellectual and moral nourishment from a thousand sources—radio, television, books, and newspapers. "In the days of God, so to speak," Prince Philip noted, "everyone was seen as equal in the sight of God. This made for anti-racialism. But take away God and we have to revert to tribalism again."

Not only does the Bible tell us that men were made by God and in God's image, but that all men also stand guilty before God. This is a common teaching in both the Old Testament and the New Testament. Isaiah confessed, "All we like sheep have gone astray, we have turned everyone to his own way" (Isaiah 53:6), while Paul plainly indicted the whole human race, Jew and pagan alike, "For all have sinned and come short of the glory of God" (Romans 3:23). A spiritual disease infects every race of men.

One glaring result of man's spiritual rebellion against God is racism. This rebellion is dramatized in Genesis 11, where we find the story of the Tower of Babel. Men decided to build a city with its top in the heavens to express their spiritual arrogance. When the Lord saw the pride of man He confused their languages so that they could not understand one another's speech, and He scattered them over the face of the earth. This act of God at Babel was a punishment for man's pride. It was also a preventive measure to protect man from destroying himself with some kind of absolute sinful power.

There are many people who believe that the Bible teaches that black men are especially cursed by God. For example, I have heard people say the Negroes are descended from Ham, one of Noah's sons, and that God condemned them to be slaves forever. A careful reading of Genesis 9 explodes this theory. Noah fell into a drunken stupor one day and one of his sons, Ham, saw his father as he lay naked in his tent. Ham told his two brothers outside, apparently in a disrespectful manner. The other brothers took a garment, and walked backward and covered the nakedness of their father; they turned their faces away so they would not see their father's nakedness. When Noah awoke he realized how Ham had shamed him. He pronounced a curse upon one of Ham's sons, Canaan, and said that he would be a slave to his brothers. Racists around the world have twisted this passage to fit their own prejudices, saying that the black man is descended from Canaan. Actually, however, it was Cush, another son of Ham, not Canaan, from whom the Ethiopians, the Africans, descended. So the theory of the black man's curse is a flimsy falsehood, completely without foundation.

It's worth noting that the Old Testament as well as the New condemns racism. Numbers 12 relates that when Moses married a Cushite woman, an Ethiopian, his brother and sister, Aaron and Miriam, despised and spoke against Moses. Apparently they despised this interracial marriage. In answer, God judged Aaron and Miriam for their prejudice and caused leprosy to come upon them!

Certainly God gives different gifts and different privileges to different people. The Bible does not flatten all men out in a kind of bland equality. As Jesus taught, some men may have one talent, some two, some may have five or ten. Yet the Scripture teaches over and over that "God is not a respecter of persons." That principle is repeated at least eight different times in the Bible. It applies to man's acceptance with God. Peter said, "Truly I perceive that God shows no partiality but in every nation anyone who hears him and does what is right is acceptable to him" (Acts 10:34-35). It should determine the nature of relationships between Christian masters and slaves, employers and employees. Paul taught, "Masters . . . forbear threatening, knowing that he who is both their master and yours is in heaven and there is no partiality with him" (Ephesians 6:9). It applies to the judgment of God "for the wrongdoer will be paid back for the wrong he has done and there is no partiality" (Colossians 3:25). This principle guides the treatment of the poor in the Christian church. "My brethren, show no partiality as you hold the faith of our Lord Jesus Christ, the Lord of glory" (James 2:1).

The Scripture also tells us that there is one Savior for all men, Jesus Christ, and that the way of salvation is open to all, "for there is no distinction between Jew and Greek; the same Lord is Lord of all and bestows his riches upon all who call upon him. For every one who calls upon the name of the Lord will be saved" (Romans 10:12-13). In the times of Jesus there was no greater division than that between Jew and Gentile. Yet Paul could say that Christ reconciled both "to God and one body through the cross, thereby bringing the hostility to an end" (Ephesians 2:16). God transcended the differences by giving to Jew and Gentile a new status. All blood-bought believers were brothers in Christ.

In our Crusades around the world we have seen black and white, young and old, the rich with their minks and the poor with their shabby clothes coming forward to trust the same Savior. The ground is surely level at the foot of the cross! At a time of grave crisis in Alabama President Lyndon Johnson requested Billy Graham to hold meetings across the length and breadth of the state. Canceling other plans, Dr. Graham did so. Interracial meetings, some of them the first in history, were held in cities large and small. I remember sitting in the Crampton Bowl in Montgomery. Half the crowd was black and half was white. There together singing the same hymns, saying the same prayers to the same God, there was a unity. One aristocratic white lady came forward at the invitation to stand by the platform. A Negro lady came and counseled her. Afterward someone asked the white lady if she minded a Negro counseling her. Her reply: "Did a Negro counsel me?" She had become oblivious to the difference of race in the light of Christ.

The Bible also teaches that there is one Holy Spirit who baptizes all who have been born again into the one body of Christ, the church (1 Corinthians 12:13). As a devout Jewish boy, Paul had been taught to thank God that he had not been born a Gentile, a slave, or a woman. But when he became a free man in Christ he wrote to the Galatians, "There is neither Jew nor Greek, neither slave nor free, neither male nor female, for you are all one in Christ Jesus" (Galatians 3:28). Racial superiority was gone; "There is neither Jew nor Greek." Every race, color, and language was included in the offer of salvation through faith in Christ. Class superiority was gone; "There is neither slave nor free." Pride of face or grace or race had disappeared in a common loyalty to Jesus! Sexual superiority was gone; "There is neither male nor female." Feminists should take note: Paul, whom many supposed to have been an anti-female, asserted that in Christ male and female were one and equal, and he did this in a world in which women were despised and often exploited.

Of course, all this doesn't mean that racial, social, and sexual differences are literally gone. After one becomes a Christian he is still black or white, illiterate or highly educated, man or woman. When we say that Christ has nullified these distinctions, we don't mean that they're not there. We mean that they don't matter. They still exist but no longer do they create any barriers to fellowship.

Racism was a widespread problem in the ancient world. For example, the Fourth Gospel tells us that "the Jews have no dealings with the Samaritans" (John 4:9). A wall of bitterness and hatred stood between the two races. The shortest route for Jews to take from Galilee to Judea was through Samaria, but they habitually took a roundabout route to avoid facing their enemies. When the Jews wanted to insult Jesus they said He was a Samaritan and had a demon. Jesus refused to go along with this racial prejudice. He deliberately went to Samaria on different occasions. When He healed ten lepers He reminded men that the only one who returned to say thanks was a Samaritan. It was a Samaritan who was the hero of His parable of the man who fell among thieves. In broad daylight He talked with a Samaritan woman of bad reputation by the well of Sychar (John 4:7 ff.). His evangelistic orders to His disciples included Samaria in their itinerary (Acts 1:8).

It was not easy for the early Christians to follow Jesus' teachings and practice wholeheartedly. There was a struggle before Samaritans and other Gentiles were admitted into full fellowship. A top-level investigating committee had to be sent to make sure the Samaritan believers were genuine Christians (Acts 8:14).

All this should be a lesson to us that prejudice does not automatically leave at conversion. Long after Peter began to follow Jesus, God had an assignment for him to go tell the good news to a God-fearing Roman Army officer named Cornelius. Knowing that Peter, as a Jew, would rebel against contact with a Gentile, He first sent Peter a vision of a great sheet let down from Heaven with all kinds of animals and birds and told him to eat. Peter refused to eat what he as a Jew had been taught was "unclean food" until God said, "Peter, what God says is kosher you must not call common!" Peter had to learn that God was cleansing and accepting Gentiles as well as Jews, that God "shows no partiality" but accepts those "in every nation who fear him" (Acts 10:35).

Many Christians have yet to let Christ revolutionize racial attitudes. Like Peter we need to have the Holy Spirit change this area of our lives. Paul Rees tells of meeting an American sergeant in Japan who had been trying to witness to another sergeant, a black man, about Christ. Three times the other man was nearly ready to accept Christ but each time he stopped short. At last the Negro sergeant disclosed what was holding him back. Painfully, he uncovered his real hesitation. "Look," he said, "if I accept Christ I can go to chapel with you here in Japan. Right? But can I go to church with you when we get back home?" The Christian sergeant was stopped short. He knew that his friend would not be welcome back home and he said, "Dr. Rees, God had to bring me all the way to Japan to see that there is a relation between Jesus Christ and this race thing."

What can I do? People all over America and the world are asking that question as we face the pent-up boiling forces of racial turbulence.

We can rejoice and be glad that God has made a colorful world. There are 88 keys on the piano. Play only the white keys, you get some music. Play only the black keys, you get other music. But you have to play both, black and white, to have harmony and great music. So God has a plan for all the races. The black man doesn't need to be made in the image of the white man or the white man in the image of the black. We all need to learn by the grace of God to reflect His image!

Equally important is the frank facing of racism in our own hearts. Few people will admit to being outright bigots any more. We like to protest, I don't have any prejudice! But inside, each of us does have areas of deliberate misunderstanding. Sin affects each of us, cuts us off from God, makes us insecure; so we try to gain a feeling of security by cutting someone else down, perhaps someone of another race. This is a subtle process that infects each of us. The first step in really coming to know the power of Jesus Christ is a genuine honesty, an honesty that is willing to let God search our hearts and show us in our own lives areas where we need cleansing.

We must learn to accept freely the fact that God accepts us as we are when we come to Him in faith and let the "blood of Jesus Christ, God's Son, cleanse us from all sin." God can wipe away the stain of prejudice. A lot of so-called race relations have been built on guilt, fear, and manipulation by both sides. This is a poor basis for understanding. Guilt covers over what's inside us and festers into fear and resentment that poisons. Grace, on the other hand, opens us up and produces genuine love.

And further, we can let God show each of us a place where we can build a bridge. This isn't a matter of running helter-skelter in a hundred different directions. It's a matter of quietly letting the Holy Spirit direct each one of us to do what lies within our power. This will mean sharing the Christ who can change men's hearts. It will mean supporting laws that oppose all kinds of discriminations. Laws can't make people love one another but they can help to prevent flagrant injustice. We can make friends with those of other races. Church leaders can arrange programs of exchange visits with people from churches of other races and make sure that their own churches are known to be open to all races in Christ's name. Businessmen and union officials can help open up places for individuals from minority groups. If we want to act, there is something for each of us to do!

Housing is a most crucial area in which Christians may exert their influence. Many blacks feel that the key to solution of other racial problems—such as school integration—lies in the availability of good housing to those who can afford it regardless of race. However, the phrase "open housing" arouses emotion and fear in some people more than almost any other aspect of the race situation. The unscrupulous salesman will prey on such fears to conjure up visions of black "invasions" and plummeting "property values." In such a situation, what will the Christian do? Will he too panic and run? Will he sound off as a self-righteous saint who has all the answers and none of the concerns of his neighbors? Or will he be able to pose a constructive alternative?

Often Christians acting together can do more than an individual. One of my colleagues, Howard Jones, tells two stories illustrating how two churches exerted their influence on housing in diametrically opposite directions. In the first instance, a friend took him by to see a beautiful large church plant in a major city. Once these buildings had been owned by a large white congregation with an outstanding record for support of world missions. Now on the steeple was painted a Muslim crescent. When the first Negro (a well-to-do professional man) moved into that neighborhood, the church panicked and put their property up for sale. But they were unable to find a church group to buy it and finally sold it to a real estate agent who in turn sold it to the Black Muslims! The congregation moved out to the faraway suburbs and built another expensive plant. Ironically, a week after the dedication of the new sanctuary the first black family moved into their new neighborhood, which raises the interesting question as to how long they will be able to cut and run!

In complete contrast is another congregation, largely white, just as evangelical as the first church, in a similar neighborhood but with a vision, faith and courage that is entirely different. The minister of this church invited Howard Jones to come for a Sunday evening presentation on the racial situation from a Scriptural stand-point. After discussion and prayer the people of this church decided to tackle the problem before it arose. They appointed representatives who went to the real estate firms of the area, told them of their intention to stay and minister where the church was, and courteously requested their cooperation in avoiding any "flight mentality" or scare-mongering. What the future holds for these people who can predict? Social change and pressure may be so rapid that regardless of what they do the racial makeup of their church and neighborhood will have to alter. Yet which church will be judged as most faithful to its Lord? Two buildings answer that question: one vacated by Christ's followers who found the price of staying too high, crowned now with Mohammad's symbol; the other where the Cross is still held high.

Jesus Christ is working a "quiet revolution" in racial affairs. Newark, New Jersey, was called the most dangerous city in America after the recent riots. But in Newark lives Bill Iverson, a man who was burdened to reach youth in the ghettos with the love of Christ. As a first step he bought a lunch counter across from one of the biggest inner-city high schools. Over many months he reached out in friendship to the young people who came in, winning their trust. His witness across the counter resulted in many of them finding Christ. In the aftermath of his spiritual work, street academies were founded for school dropouts. When Newark was blazing in the terrible riots of 1967, the one shop in that block that was not burned out with a Molotov cocktail was that lunch counter. In the middle of the riots both National Guardsmen and black ghetto residents sat drinking coffee! God had used His man as a bridge across troubled waters.

On April 4, 1968, Martin Luther King, Jr., was cut down by a sniper's bullet on a motel balcony in Memphis. In the aftermath of this assassination a huge wave of vengeance battered the United States. On the other side of the continent that wave engulfed and killed another Martin, a white bus driver named Martin Whitted. At the end of his run in a lonely section of Hunters Point in San Francisco, eleven black youths pulled him from his bus, savagely battered him, and left him mortally wounded. Tension and countertension rose in the black and white communities. Ugly rumors of violence began to circulate. Fear that the two murders would mean yet more violent outbursts settled on a large part of the community. Then Dixie Whitted, Martin's widow, asked to appear on television. Quietly she spoke of her love for her husband and of her faith in Christ. She told the people she knew how many of them felt but she pleaded with them to refrain from any violence and to be peacemakers instead. Through the power of Jesus Christ, she said, she had no bitterness or hate. She knew that many who were watching wanted not retaliation but reconciliation. Her little community needed recreational facilities for all the young people, and if they wanted to do something, those who were watching could send gifts to build this facility as a memorial to her husband.

The effect was electric! Cynical television crewmen cried and a Stanford coed called in to say that her whole life and attitude had been changed by this Christian witness. At the funeral in St. Mark's Lutheran Church, Pastor Ross Hidy said, "When I married Dixie and Martin six years ago there were two Negroes, friends of theirs, at the wedding." And when he had finished three blacks and three whites picked up the coffin and carried it out.

The time has come for a new slogan. We have heard about law power, learning power, earning power. These have their places. So does "black power" when it means that the black man must forge a place for himself and learn to have a justifiable pride in his own history and race. But we need another rallying cry today, "Christ power!" That's the power that can make us love each other. That's the power that can help the white man to turn away from hatred or bigotry or fear. That's the power that can guide the black man or the brown man or the red man away from resentment to use his power with grace and wisdom.

"Christ power!" For the authentic Christ offers us the one way to turn from our hatred, bigotry, and fear; the one way genuinely to build a community of love; the one way to let God flesh out His power in our redeemed humanity, be it black, white, or brown.

8 EARTHSHAKER

Elijah, the fiery Old Testament prophet, once had an encounter with the false prophets of Baal. He challenged them to a contest of their gods versus Jehovah. Whichever deity could cause fire to fall from heaven and consume a bull laid on an altar would be recognized as the true God. From morning until noon Baal's prophets called on their idol: "O Baal, answer us!" But no one answered. At noon it is recorded Elijah mocked them, saying, "Cry aloud, for he is a god; either he is musing or he has gone aside or he is on a journey, or perhaps he is asleep and must be awakened" (I Kings 18:26 f.). Then Elijah prayed and the fire of the Lord Jehovah fell and consumed the bull.

Christians today are the frequent targets of the same taunts Elijah tossed at Baal's prophets: "What's happened to your God? Is He asleep? has He gone away?"

If we are tempted to wonder whether God has indeed abdicated, then we must recapture the vision of God as the Great Activist. Ponder the pictures we have seen of the tiny band of Christians from the book of Acts: What impression comes across? It is that of a revolutionary God, releasing revolutionary power through revolutionary community in revolutionary action. Here are still the essential ingredients in the Christian recipe for revolution.

"The great fact is revolution," says a prominent theologian. Quite true. But the Christian has to start further back. The greater fact is God! Not the word "god," but the God who is really there.

"I believe in God the Father Almighty, Maker of heaven and earth." We gladly confess that faith. But do we also believe in God the Father Almighty—Shaker of heaven and earth? One of our evangelical slogans says, "God is still on the throne." But is this more than a cliché? Are we men and women who share the vision of John, "Then I saw a new heaven and a new earth . . . and He

who sat upon the throne said, 'Behold, I make all things new.' "
(Revelation 21:1–5)? Or have we lost our poise because somehow
we feel that our world has gotten beyond God's control?

When those early Christians were arrested for disturbing the
peace they lifted their voices in prayer. Quoting from their Bibles
they said,

Sovereign Lord, who didst make the heaven and the earth and the
sea and everything in them, who by the mouth of our father David,
thy servant, did say by the Holy Spirit, "Why did the gentiles rage
and the peoples imagine vain things? The kings of the earth set themselves in array, and the rulers were gathered together, against the Lord
and against His Anointed" (Acts 4:24–26).

According to the Psalm from which they quoted, when men
rebel against God's authority,

He who sits in the heavens laughs; the Lord has them in dersion.
Then He will speak to them in His wrath, and terrify them in His
    fury, saying,
"I have set my king on Zion, my holy hill" (Psalm 2:4–6).

These early Christian revolutionaries had implicit confidence
that their God was at the master controls of history. Rebellion
against His rule was bound to fail. He laughed from heaven at the
empty posturings and vain plans of those who set themselves to
topple Him from His throne. The rushes and changes of history
were under His supervision. When Jeremiah saw the vision of the
seething cauldron the Lord said, "Look, I am calling all of the
tribes of the kingdoms of the north . . . and they shall come."
Heathen nations and kings were his personnel. If the Jews would
not carry out God's plans then He would use the heathen. He calls
Assyria "The rod of my anger, the staff of my fury" (Isaiah 10:5).
Unbelievers have been raised up by God to chastise believers.

He describes Cyrus, the king of Persia, as "My anointed" and
says to him.

For the sake of my servant Jacob, and Israel my chosen, I will call
you by your name, I surname you, though you do not know me.
I am the Lord and there is no other, besides me there is no God;
I gird you, though you do not know me, that men may know, from

the rising of the sun, and from the west, that there is none besides me; I am the Lord, and there is no other. I form light and create darkness, I make weal and create woe. I am the Lord, who do all these things (Isaiah 45:4-7).

Cyrus was God's unconscious tool.

When Habakkuk cried out to God for help because of the violence, wickedness, and perversion of justice, God answered, "Look among the nations and see; wonder and be astounded. For I am doing a work in your days that you would not believe if told. For lo, I am raising the Chaldeans, that bitter and hasty nation . . ." (Habakkuk 1:5-6).

Assyrians, Chaldeans, Persians! Violence, tumult, upheaval! All of this permitted by the God of the Bible! He is not dead. He is not sick. He is not asleep. He is the Lord of history, who is working out His purposes as year succeeds to year. He who made Cyrus his unconscious tool is not dismayed by Mao Tsetung! This God will take the wild rage of the ghettos, the apathy of the suburbs, the unrest on the campus, the nightmare of Vietnam, and weave these tangled threads into the fabric of His plan.

This Lord to whom the early Christians prayed was not only the Lord of the past. He was the Lord of their present—the God of the Now Generation, if you will. They asked Him for current action and current power, "And *now*, Lord, look upon her threats and grant to thy servants to speak thy word with boldness, while thou stretcheth out thy hand to heal. . . . And when they had prayed, the place in which they were gathered together was shaken" (Acts 4:29-31). Shaken by the Lord of Hosts who said through Haggai, "Once again, in a little while, I will shake the heavens and the earth and the sea and the dry land; and I will shake all nations, so that the treasures of all nations will come in, and I will fill this house with splendor" (Haggai 2:6-7).

In a day of revolution, Christian outreach must begin with a new vision of the revolutionary God who is shaking all nations so that their treasures may come in, so that from every people and tongue and tribe and nation may come the parade of valued lives, human treasures, redeemed by the blood of the lamb, and giving glory to God.

When we see our world shaken as never before, it is not a time to despair. It is a time to watch God opening doors that have never before been opened. A black Ph.D. who is working in the New York ghettos told me of the upheaval that is coming in the inner city. Then he made this significant comment, "The present revolutionary ferment in the city, when people have come to the end of their resources, is a perfect opportunity for preaching the gospel."

Donald McGavran, who heads the Institute of Church Growth at Fuller Theological Seminary, made the same point to a seminar of missionaries. He said, "If you were given the choice between living in a time free of revolution or in an era being shaken to the foundations by it, choose to be alive in a time of revolution." While sudden change may sometimes close doors to the Gospel, he explained, it often happens that a world in revolution finds a change in people's responsiveness to the Word of God.

Dramatic illustrations of this have been seen in our time. In the time since Sukarno fell in Indonesia, tens of thousands of people have been swept into the kingdom of God. Since 1960 the Congo has been chronically gripped by terror and turmoil. But in the last several years the Christ For All campaign has seen thousands of Congolese won to Christ. In Church Growth Through Evangelism in Depth. Malcolm Bradshaw notes that this campaign came "at a decisive moment when change was seemingly inevitable in the revolutionary climate of the country . . . the hand of the Sovereign God has prepared Congo for this moment of unprecedented receptivity."

God has not been caught cat napping by revolution. The God who permitted Assyrians to chastise Israel can allow Communism both to chastise the Christian church for our lack of compassion and our sloth, and even to prepare the way for the Gospel. Some China watchers, for example, believe that some day its evangelization will be far easier because the Communist regime has broken up many of the old patterns of the past, put in a simple system of writing, and eliminated many of the dangers of travel. This is not to excuse their sins or to approve of their values. It is to recognize that God can make the wrath of men praise

Him! As Joseph told his brothers who had sold him into slavery, "You meant it for evil, but God meant it for good."

Just as we Christians must catch a new vision of the revolutionary God, so we must also begin to evangelize today by confronting non-Christians with His reality. Francis Schaeffer, the founder of the L'Abri Community in Switzerland and evangelist to students and intellectuals, has driven home this point in his book, *The God Who Is There*. He holds that there is little use in pressing the plan of salvation upon someone who does not believe in the reality of God or acknowledge his guilt. Says Schaeffer, "We must never forget that the first part of the gospel is not 'accept Christ as Saviour,' but 'God is there.'"

Christian faith, Schaeffer continues, means that a man must bow twice. First, he must bow metaphysically, he must acknowledge that he is a creature before the infinite personal creator. Second, he needs to bow morally, to acknowledge that he is a sinner and that he is guilty before this holy God.

There are many today who will deny the reality of this God and yet profess to be concerned for change in the direction of human values. Christians must have genuine appreciation for their concern, yet also confront them with the question: what rationale can there be for any significant change of human values apart from the reality of this God?

Unique to biblical thinking is its view of history. It is from the Bible that we derive the conviction that history has a purpose and a goal, like an arrow shot toward a target. History can be changed because it is not the plaything of blind fates, but the result of a real dialogue between God and man. Darwin, Freud, and Marx, who so strongly helped to shape the modern mind, all stressed that man is a prisoner of forces outside his control. The world is like a great Las Vegas—a gamble without meaning— unless we believe that the God who began the human story can intervene again and make a difference.

The same holds true with human personality. Many of the non-Christian revolutionaries of our day claim to have high regard for man and to be seeking more humane and just societies. But again we must press them. Who is this man you are concerned to help? A sophisticated animal? An early-model computer? Or a soul made with the capacity to relate to God? If man is just an animal or a machine, then why not manipulate him like one?

I talked with a man who visited the barricades at the Sorbonne in Paris when the students rioted there. He and some other Christians had gone to distribute gospels and to witness for Christ. A huge man with a black bushy beard accosted him and demanded to know what he was doing. My friend explained and the man said, "When we come to revolution we'll put you Christians in your place." My friend then asked him who he was and what he was doing. It turned out that he was an airline pilot between flights. He had come to take part in the demonstrations. "I'm protesting this rotten lousy world," he exclaimed. "Why?" my friend demanded. "Do you believe in God?" With a snort of disgust the man made it very clear that he was an atheist. The Christian pointed out to him that he had just made a value judgment. He had said that this was a rotten and lousy world. On what basis, he asked, did he make such a value judgment and say there was any difference between right and wrong if there was no God?

For some time they debated. And then my friend took a different tack. "Tell me," he said, "is there anyone you love?" The pilot said no. "Are you married?" He replied that he was. Did he love his wife? No, he did not. Was there nobody that he loved? The man bowed his head in deep thought for a moment and then quietly said, "Yes, there is. There's a woman by whom I've had a child. And she's dying with leukemia. And I love her."

My friend walked right up to him and shouted in his face, "Forget her. She's worthless. She's nothing! Forget her!" The big pilot doubled his fist and was ready to knock him down when my friend backed away, held up his hand and said, "Wait, I didn't mean that. Of course, that's not what she is, but on your principles she is only a bunch of chemicals. What makes her worth loving? Why do you love her?" At the end of their discussion a very thoughtful pilot walked away with a Gospel of John in his hand, prepared to read it.

Unless we believe that man is the creation of a personal infinite God, there is no adequate reason to believe that love and communication and human responsibility have any meaning whatsoever. Erich Fromm is right when he says, "The problem in the last century was that God was dead. The problem in this century is that man is dead." For if God is dead, then so is man—hopelessly so!

But while the church confesses her faith in this revolutionary God, we must ask: Do we demonstrate before the world what we confess? Is there anything about us and our movement that the world cannot explain away, about which it must say, This is God at work?

Two attitudes characterized the early Christians, both of which grew out of their confidence in God. There was a humility with which, as one, they came before God in prayer. And there was the boldness with which they came before men in their witness.

If our Christian work is marked by presumption and worldly confidence on the one hand, or if it shows fear and an apologetic attitude on the other, then we are not working in the power of the living God. We cannot serve God in the might of our organization, our clever words, or our shiny personalities. It is not by these things but "by my Spirit, says the Lord," that God's task goes forward.

No church has ever yet been a church of revolutionary power that has not been a church of prayer. At a conference held in Leysin, Switzerland, late in 1969, representatives of the major "saturation evangelism" movements from around the world were present. It was reported that wherever the Spirit of God is moving in unusual and transforming power today one of the common factors has been a new emphasis on prayer, both individual and united. In Korea, for example, the average church member goes to a prayer meeting every morning at his church before he begins his daily work. How many of our churches in the West even have any vital prayer meeting any more?

Because the task is so great, we must fall on our faces before God in earnest prayer. Because God is so great, we must rise and stand on our feet and move into the world in aggressive witness and work, demonstrating that "greater is He that is in you than he that is in the world."

"The future is ours, comrades," cries the dedicated Marxist, and gives himself in self-sacrifice to implement the vision of a classless society. "The future is God's, brothers," should be our response as Christians, as we give ourselves with no less zeal to the vision of the kingdom of God.

9 REVOLUTION PLUS ONE

The *Toronto Globe and Mail* recently carried a feature article by an Asian correspondent on the little red book that is changing China. The red book, of course, comprises "The Thoughts of Chairman Mao." The correspondent told of seeing people reading it everywhere he went in China. A farmer stood reading it beside his plow. A railway worker held it up as the train passed by. A group of soldiers sat on the ground reading aloud from it. Three taxi drivers quoted from it to each other. Four little girls stood by the curb and waved the red books at the cars going by.

Chinese Communist leaders have compiled this book, consisting of four hundred quotations from Mao Tse-tung, and through it they mean to "revolutionize" the thinking of seven hundred million Chinese. But these quotations from Mao are not for native consumers only. According to the New China News Agency, they are as necessary "as the sun, air, food and water to the revolutionary people of the world." Foreign language editions published since the Chinese cultural revolution began have sold well over five million copies. One Chinese Communist leader says, "Once Mao Tse-tung's thought is grasped by the broad masses, it becomes an inexhaustible source of strength and a spiritual atom bomb of infinite power."

At this point, as Christians, we need to ask ourselves some acute questions and answer as honestly as we can. Have we lost faith in the power of God to change men? Often we quote that great text, "If any man is in Christ, he is a new creation." Is this just another slogan that we repeat like parrots? Or do we really believe that God releases into human lives that same fantastic, transforming power by which he raised Jesus Christ from the dead? Confidence in the revolutionary power of the Gospel

led the apostles to invade the power centers of their day. Paul
went to Rome saying, "I'm not ashamed of the gospel of Christ,
for it is the power of God unto salvation to everyone that believes" (Romans 1:16).

Do *we* think that *man's* power is all we have?

Can Jesus Christ really change men? This is no academic
question. The shape of our task depends on it.

The church stands with all mankind at a common crossroads
sharing a common concern: Which way de we go to make a
new world? There are some who say, "*Learn*—education is the way.
Some say, "*Earn*—economic development will solve our problems."
Some voices are crying, "*Burn*—society is so corrupt we must
destroy it." There is truth in all of this. But Jesus Christ says,
"*Turn*. Be converted. Put your trust in God. Seek first His will.
Then you can be part of the new world God is making."

Most revolutions fail because they are not revolutionary enough.
They fail to grasp the heart of the problem, which is the problem
of the human heart. Jesus said, "What comes out of a man
is what defiles a man. For from within, out of the heart of man,
come evil thoughts, fornication, theft, murder, adultery, coveting,
wickedness, deceit, licentiousness, envy, slander, pride, foolishness.
All these evil things come from within, and they defile a man"
(Mark 7:20–23). This is why revolution without regeneration
tends to forge new chains. As an old French proverb has it,
"The more things change, the more they remain the same." So
these revolutions are aptly named: they revolve! They throw
out one set of sinners and put in another set. As Christians
we believe that we need a revolution that gets to the root of our
trouble. We dare not separate our efforts to change things outside man from our need to change what is inside man.

Recently the newspapers carried a series of follow-up articles
on the 230 University of California students who were arrested
during the Berkeley free speech demonstrations in 1964. It was
interesting to note their attitudes today. Fifty per cent thought
their participation in those demonstrations had made them more
radical now than they were before. Twenty-one per cent felt that
their radical attitudes gained then had been erased by time.
(It's interesting to note that most of these people had strong re-

ligious views, believing, for example, that the Bible is "God's Word.") Twenty-nine per cent said that they had been highly radical before the disruptions, and still were.

One young man who had demonstrated, protested, marched, sat in, and been jailed made an interesting comment. He indicated that he had lost his faith in political demonstrations and instead was looking for some other way. "We complain about the establishment, he said, "but the establishment is just a group of people. To change the policy you have to change the people. If the people who make the policy are unhappy or tense or out of touch with human values, then no matter what you do, if they haven't changed within themselves and become more peaceful, the policy they make isn't going to change."

No matter how you mix up rotten apples they'll not make a good pie. And no matter how you relate imperfect human beings they will not make a perfect society. I believe it was Churchill who once said that the root error of Communism and of all utopianism was an overoptimistic view of human nature. A great deal of the frustration, the pent-up anger, and the hostility of our time come from expectations that have been built up on naïve views of human nature. As Elton Trueblood incisively notes in *The New Man for Our Time,*

The Christian faith, when understood, helps to avoid the bitterness of disillusionment by making it clear in advance that there will be no Utopia. The impossibility of Utopia follows logically from the chronic character of human sin, which infects the planners in the same way that it infects those for whom the new social order is planned.

Every revolutionary movement must come to grips with the fact of sin. What we need is a more radical, more revolutionary revolution that understands that before there can be real revolution there must be genuine repentance.

By now we should have learned that progress—educational, economic, scientific, or political—important as it is, is not in itself sufficient to bring about the necessary changes in our world. The near civil war on our university campuses should have exploded the notion of education as a panacea. The week that

Apollo 11 went to the moon there was probably more optimism shown than ever before about what man can do. Yet Cape Kennedy itself is a symbol of our paradoxical age, for the moonport area has the highest divorce rate and the second highest alcoholism rate in the entire United States! Consider also the plight of the brilliant South African surgeon, who could replace a man's heart but could not repair his own marriage.

Former Ambassador George Kennan recognized the ultimate problem in a debate with young radicals. In *Democracy and the Student Left*, he writes of

a vitally important truth—a truth that the Marxists, among others, have never brought themselves to recognize—namely, that the decisive seed of evil in this world is not in social and political institutions, and not even, as a rule, in the will or iniquities of statesmen, but simply in the weakness and the imperfections of the human soul itself, and by that I mean literally every soul, including my own, and that of the student militant at the gates.

Christians are often accused of undue pessimism and always harping on sin. But paradoxically, only when sin is faced as a moral reality is there hope! If man is the prisoner of his circumstances, if the human dilemma rises from a wrong combination of chemicals, or from psychological factors beyond man's control, then man is just programmed wrong and we should abandon ourselves to evil. But if the cause of our dilemma is a moral one, rebellion against God, then there can be an answer from God's side.

Among other things, the Christian doctrine of God and of sin gives us a real basis for a true rebellion against evil in the world. Albert Camus, the French existentialist, holds out two options in his novel, *The Plague*. In effect he argues that we can either be Christians and go along with evil because God wills it, or we can be atheists and rebel against it. That is a false antithesis. The atheist may fight evil, but he has no adequate moral basis for judging it to be wrong. It is only the believer who can really rebel against evil. A Christian can stand against evil because God is against it!

Moses was one of history's greatest freedom fighters. It was he who led the exodus of the Jewish people from slavery in Egypt to freedom. But Moses' first efforts to be a freedom fighter were a dismal failure. He had to learn that there was no shortcut to freedom. Like many of the students and young people today who are engaged in the struggle for freedom and justice, Moses was a member of the establishment, the privileged class. The son of Jewish slaves, he had been adopted by the daughter of the ruler of Egypt and had grown up with all the advantages of the palace. One day he decided to visit his own people, the Jews. Seeing one of them being beaten by an Egyptian, he defended the oppressed man by striking and killing the Egyptian. He supposed that his brothers would understand that God was delivering them by his hand, but they did not. The next day he saw them quarreling among themselves and tried to reconcile them. "Men," he called out, "you are brothers. Why do you wrong each other?" But the man who was wronging his neighbor said, "Who made you a ruler and a judge over us? Do you want to kill me as you killed the Egyptian yesterday?" At this, Moses fled and lived for years as an exile in the desert.

Like many young idealists today, Moses was ready to strike a revolutionary blow for freedom. But his ideals took a hard whack when he discovered, first, that they did not immediately bow down in gratitude to accept his leadership, and second, that the Jews could be just as selfish as the Egyptians. The oppressed were as capable of injustice as the oppressors and Moses had to face this truth. Evil is not just in social structures; evil is in people.

Forty years later Moses had an encounter with God in the lonely desert. Seeing a bush on fire, he drew near and the Lord spoke out of the bush and said, "I am the God of your father . . . take off the shoes from your feet, for the place where you are standing is holy ground. I have surely seen the ill treatment of my people that are in Egypt and heard their groaning and I have come down to deliver them. And now, come, I will send you to Egypt."

At the burning bush Moses learned that God was as concerned with oppression, injustice, and slavery as he was. God's plan was to send Moses as the great liberator, but Moses was of no use to God until he came face to face with God's holiness and sovereign power and with his own frailty and sin. That encounter in the desert changed Moses from a man who was merely a freedom fighter into a man of faith who could be a freedom builder. It was a fairly easy thing to strike a violent blow and shed blood. It was a far more difficult thing to have the kind of spiritual vision that could take a demoralized crew of slaves and mold them into a nation under God.

If we are to know genuine freedom, at least in a limited sense, throughout the world today, we need a whole new generation of freedom builders like Moses. We need young men and women, and mature men and women, who can be stirred when they see people oppressed and suffering because they know that God is stirred. We need those who will dedicate their lives to setting people free from the slavery of hunger and disease and ignorance and prejudice. But most of all we need freedom builders who can call upon the power that can set people free from the inner slavery of sin.

At the heart of the Christian strategy for change is conversion. Jesus said, "Unless you turn (convert) become like children you cannot enter the kingdom of God." The Christian idea of conversion isn't basically a certain kind of an emotional experience. It means turning around from the slavery of sin to the service of God. At a Church and Society Conference held in Geneva, Dr. W. A. Visser 't Hooft said that while Christians know changes must take place in social and political structures, "There is a deeper 'revolution' required, namely, that of man himself as he turns around from egocentricity to the service of God."

Our Gospel claims that Almighty God came into human history to liberate human nature. He came to do for us what we could never do for ourselves. By the supernatural birth of Jesus Christ, God has begun a new humanity into which we may enter by a new birth. By the death of Jesus Christ for our sins, God has made it possible to wipe the slate clean, and to free those who believe from the crippling paralysis of guilt. By the risen life of Jesus Christ, shared with us through the Holy Spirit, God enables us to shake off our moral failure. And in the community of forgiven and redeemed men God gives us a place where we can foretaste the new wine of God's new world.

This Christian conversion is so revolutionary because it is so complete. When a man meets Jesus Christ, God begins to heal all his broken relationships, to put him right with God, with himself, and with his fellow man. Salvation is a three-dimensional affair. Today, when our churches are being torn apart between the so-called "soul savers" at one pole and the so-called "social reformers" at the other, it's absolutely imperative that we keep in view the completeness of the Gospel and resist the temptation of both extremes.

When Abraham Vereide, the founder of International Christian Leadership, died recently, someone described his vision in terms that should be true of the entire church, "For him, a scheme to reconstruct society which ignored the redemption of the individual was unthinkable; but a doctrine to save sinning men with no aim to transform them into crusaders against social sin was equally unthinkable."

Is this spiritual revolution really relevant to the needs of our day? It is, tremendously so, when men face our world with two attitudes. At the one extreme is the violent revolutionary; at the other is the diehard defender of the status quo. The revolutionary thinks that everything is so bad that anything would be better. The old order must be totally destroyed. Hate infects his motives, and rebellion without compassion is a poor foundation for human relationships. The diehard, on the other hand, is often motivated by fear. His security is tied into the past. If change starts, he wonders, where will it ever stop?

Hate and fear exist in each of us. Unless we can deal with them there can be no real change. But it is just here that Jesus worked the greatest change! The men who met him found hate replaced by love—because they knew Jesus loved them enough to go to a cross. They found fear replaced by hope—because Jesus was alive and coming again, and he was working in them by his Spirit and they could face the future knowing that it was in Jesus' hands.

We 20th-century Christians need to recover confidence in the revolutionary power of our Gospel, that we may give ourselves with utter abandon as our first-century forebearers did to the proclamation of this good news. Perhaps, however, we need to enter a word or two of caution at this point, lest we promise more than we can produce. Sometimes Christians have naïvely expected too much from professed conversions.

Our evangelism must be certain that conversion is authentic, a real experience and not just a word. Here we could take a page from the wisdom of the Puritans, who were careful to test professions of faith by the quality of life produced. Believing in something isn't necessarily the same as experiencing it. Jesus didn't say, "You must believe in the new birth," or "You must believe in conversion." He said, "You must be born again, you must be converted." We must learn the difference between real and artificial conversions. Some so-called religious experience only involves a redirection of hostility. Jesus didn't take all conversions at face value. "By their fruit, ye shall know them," he insisted. (Can you imagine anything that tastes worse than artificial fruit?) While we dare not be judges of ultimate spiritual reality, we can be "fruit inspectors," and test conversions by the kind of character that results. Our evangelism should be at least as concerned to discover what decisions produce, as to know what produces decisions.

Our evangelism must also insist that conversion is a beginning, not an end. Too often evangelicals have stressed a conversion experience so strongly that converts kept looking back to what happened when they were converted instead of what happens next. We have sometimes said too blithely, "The best way to change the world is to get men converted." That states an important truth, but taken by itself it can be misleading. The new birth gives the potential for personality change, but the change does not take place automatically. Conversion must lead to Christian growth.

Realism is demanded in the expectations we have for social change that results from personal conversion. As David Hubbard, the president of Fuller Theological Seminary, notes, "In our simplistic approach to the preaching of the gospel and social action, we evangelicals are very close to Roman Catholics. We are really saying that justification and sanctification take place simultaneously and are one and the same act." Let's be wary of saying that the preaching of the Gospel will solve all of society's ills. In the first place, there is no biblical warrant for believing that will happen. No permanent solution for social evil, no perfect world of justice is anticipated in the Bible before Christ returns. Quite the opposite. Jesus predicted a falling away as the end comes, and the Scripture indicates that "evil men shall wax worse and worse." The biblical view of history is that while the Gospel may spread, and good may increase as a result, there will be a terrible increasing conflict with evil until the end.

In the second place, we know that there are Bible Belts where the Gospel is preached and people are converted but where there are built-in structures and attitudes of prejudice that change very slowly. This does not mean that people are not converted, but it does mean that the Holy Spirit has a great deal of work to do in all of our hearts and minds after conversion.

Meanwhile, we can give ourselves in joyful abandonment to the task of making Christ known, because the Gospel of Christ is God's revolutionary power. What a revolution is taking place in our world today as Christ invades human personalities! Is there any other system in the world that can match transformed lives against those that Christ has touched? Think of a gang leader like Tom Skinner, whom Christ changed into an apostle of love. Think of an underworld wiretapper like Jim Vaus, who has followed Christ into youth work in the ghettos. Think of savage Auca Indians, who now love the Saviour Whose missionaries they once speared to death. Think of the comfortable, affluent suburban businessmen who have entered into the struggle for equality in their communities because of the compassion Christ gave to them. Think of addicts whom Christ has redeemed from the roller coaster of the drug scene to a spiritual trip that never ends!

Bob Dylan sings a song called "Blowin' in the Wind." It's theme is a sad lament for man's inhumanity to man. When will there be an end to selfishness and evil? How long does it take for a mountain to be eroded into the sea? Will it be that long until freedom comes? The answer to these questions, he cryptically replies, is blowing in the wind.

A Christian university student who has experienced the blowing of the wind of the Spirit in her own life has written another version of this ballad:

> How many miles will a people tread
> before they lift up their eyes?
> How many tears will they shed as they go
> before they turn to their Christ?
> How many deaths will they die all alone
> before they find new life?
> The Spirit of God is blowing in the wind.
> The answer *is* blowing in the wind!

10 BACK TO THE FUTURE

When Billy Graham was holding a Crusade in Los Angeles several years ago one clergyman complained that Mr. Graham's brand of evangelism had done serious damage, setting the church back a hundred years. Asked for his reaction, the evangelist wryly replied, "If that's true then I have failed. What I had hoped we might do is set the church back two thousand years!" The primary need of the church today is to rediscover the revolutionary secret of the first Christian community.

For the Chinese Communists the writings of Mao Tse-tung spell out their program of revolution. We Christians also have a textbook of revolution, the book called The Acts of the Apostles.

On the Day of Pentecost the Book of Acts records that the "strong driving wind" of God came upon the first Christians and "they were all filled with the Holy Spirit and began speaking in other tongues, as the (holy) Spirit gave them (power of) utterance" (Acts 2:4). Pentecost reversed Babel. At Babel men tried to become gods and the result was confusion of tongues. At Pentecost God came into men and the result was communication! God communicated revolutionary power through a revolutionary community.

In the preface of J. B. Phillips' translation of the Book of Acts he gives his impression of these early Christians. Here he writes,

The new born church, as vulnerable as any human child, having neither money, influence, nor power in the ordinary sense, is setting forth joyfully and courageously to win the pagan world for God through Christ . . . this surely is the church as it was meant to be. It is vigorous and flexible, for these are the days before it ever became fat and short of breath through prosperity, or muscle-bound by over-organization. These men did not make "acts of faith," they believed; they did not "say their prayers," they really prayed. They did not hold conferences on psychosomatic medicine, they simply healed the sick . . . there is Someone here at work besides mere human beings. It is a matter of sober, stoical fact that never before has any small body of ordinary people so moved the world that their enemies could say, with tears of rage in their eyes, that these men "have turned the world upside down"!

Here we come to one of the biggest question marks. We believe in a revolutionary God and in the Gospel of revolutionary power. But how does the church, especially the local church and its program, fit into God's revolution?

If we take the New Testament seriously, then Christianity apart from the church is a contradiction. According to Acts 2:47, "The Lord added to the church daily those who were being saved." Yet we all realize that the church, as we know it, is often our biggest hang-up in winning people to faith.

Recently I talked with a number of men involved in inner-city outreach. To each of them I posed this question, "What is your biggest obstacle?" To a man they answered, "The institutional church;" and they were speaking not with bitterness but with disappointment about both the ghetto church and the suburban church.

There is a widespread disillusionment, almost disgust, with the church. The brightest and most sensitive of our youth too often turn from the church, accusing us of having as our theme song, "I Believe in Yesterday," and of being irrelevant to the realities of the 20th century. The radical activists would scuttle the church and say, "Get into the world where the action is." Evangelicals, for different reasons, have often taken the same route. Feeling bottlenecked by the apathy of certain churches, they simply bypass them and channel their concern through a host of specialized organizations. John Mackay has compared these societies—movements such as Young Life and Campus Crusade, Inter-Varsity Christian Fellowship and Youth for Christ, the Billy Graham Crusades and a host of others—to the missionary orders in the Roman Catholic church. God has blessed these efforts and at their best they are a strong arm of the churches. Sadly there has also been on occasion an unnecessary sense of rivalry and suspicion between these movements and pastors and churches.

Certainly it is no adequate response to this age of revolution to turn the Church's evangelistic responsibility completely over to specialists. Too often we have talked of missions and evangelism as if they were adjuncts of the church's life, optional activities to be supported by those who are interested in that sort of thing. In truth, mission and evangelism are the heartbeat of the Church, for the Church lives by the Spirit of her Lord who said, "As my Father sent me into the world, so send I you" (John 20:21). When the Church ceases to evangelize, she ceases to live.

We need to wrestle with the question of what sudden and radical change is needed so that the churches themselves can be the agents of revolutionary evangelism. Men like Tom Allan in *The Face of My Parish* and Kenneth Strachan in *The Inescapable Imperative* have struggled hard with this question.

The issue is not primarily one of numbers. Numbers are important but not completely so. Two traps must be avoided: to idolize numbers and to despise numbers. There are those who measure all Christian efforts by statistics. The result has been that many feel like a pastor who groaned, when his denomination set out on a campaign to recruit a million new members, "If the next million are like the last million, may God help us!" The end of Christian witness is to glorify God, not to add up numbers, and a hundred or a thousand new converts who lead selfish and un-Christ like lives will not glorify God.

On the other hand, there are some who piously brag of their lack of numerical success, as if that proved their superior spirituality. They "outspiritualize" the New Testament because the Book of Acts constantly refers to the fact that as the Word of God went its way among men, "the number of the disciples multiplied greatly" (Acts 6:7). Church growth in numbers is by no means irrelevant. The church is both a means and an end. Every genuine statistic of a conversion means one more soldier available for the Lord's service and one more soul saved for the Savior's rejoicing. Elton Trueblood's paraphrase neatly sums up this matter: What we should be seeking is neither "the presence of crowds nor the absence of crowds" but "a new creation" in Christ.

While we can aim at greater church growth, we can also expect that the Christian church will always be a minority movement, as Jesus predicted. So we must measure evangelistic success by the quality as well as the quantity of the converts. Could anyone have predicted that the tiny handful of disciples at Pentecost would eventually conquer the mighty Roman Empire? There were only 120 of them among an estimated four million Jews in Palestine alone. That's a ratio of 1 to 33,000. It's as if there were only 6,000 believers in the entire United States. So-called minority movements have always turned out to be the most crucial because they cast the shadow of the future. One per cent of the Russians brought about the Russian Revolution. Nazism was always a minority until it was too late. A leader of the radical student Left recently told Billy Graham that they were trying to cut their movement down by two-thirds until they had a dedicated group of trained and disciplined followers who could bring about the revolution.

The crucial issue is not in fact "How big is the church?" but "What is the church?"

In the Bible, the basic idea of the church is not buildings or programs or budgets but "people"—God's redeemed people. At the very beginning of Jesus' ministry His strategy was to gather a group of men who would continue, deepen, and spread His work. Out of all His followers He chose twelve into whom He could pour His life. Mark relates that Jesus "went up into the hills and called to him those whom he desired; and they came to him. And he appointed twelve to be with him and to be sent out to preach and to have authority to cast out demons" (Mark 3:13–15).

What distinguished these men? First, they had a personal commitment to Christ. He "called those whom he desired and they came to him." Second, they had a unique fellowship in Christ. They included men of different temperaments, like impetuous Peter and quiet John, and of varied political persuasions, like Simon the Zealot, a member of the resistance, and Matthew who worked for the Roman forces of occupation. Before they met Jesus, Simon would have gladly slit Matthew's throat. But when Christ accepted them they accepted each other. Third, they had a clear mission *for* Christ. Jesus called them to "be with him" in personal fellowship, so Mark says, but also to "be sent out to preach and . . . cast out demons," to make Christ known by word and deed.

If the church today is to be the agent of revolutionary evangelism, we must be clear that by the church we mean those who have made a personal commitment to Christ. People can be trained as evangelists who have a motivation to share Christ. But if people lack this motivation no amount of training will help. What such people need is an encounter with Christ. We must seriously consider the question of what it means to have "conversion within the church." Why do so many students seem to abandon their faith when they go to college? Why do so many couples stop attending church when they move to a new city? Is it because they have only an "environmental faith" and have "oozed" into church membership without any clear commitment? How do we help people with a secondhand faith to really come alive in Christ?

Traditionally, churches have tended to face this matter of a meaningful commitment in one of two ways. There have been the "gathered" churches and there have been the "multitudinous" churches. The "gathered" church has put its emphasis on purity, discipline, high standards, the cost of commitment. Rigorous demands are made of converts before they enter into full church membership. "Multitudinous" churches, on the other hand, have taken the attitude: let all who will, come; let us open the doors of the church wide, and hope that after people get inside something will happen to them. Both have New Testament warrant for their positions. The "gathered" church remembers its Lord who spoke of taking up a cross, who underlined the cost of commitment, who said that those who followed Him must be willing to forsake all. The "multitudinous" church remembers its Savior who died on a cross for failing, fallible people, who spoke of the freedom of salvation, and who said, "Come unto me all who are heavy laden and I will give you rest."

But both groups can also fall into grave peril. The "gathered" church may raise the wall of demand so high that those on the outside despair of ever being worthy to enter, while those inside may preen themselves in pride. The "multitudinous" church may well open the door so wide that the whole concept of commitment becomes meaningless and Christian belief and behavior lose their saltiness.

Overseas the younger churches face this issue acutely. In cultures where polygamy has been the custom, for example, must a convert turn out all his wives but one in order to be a fully dedicated Christian? Some countries have experienced the so-called "people's movements" where entire families, villages, and tribes respond to the Gospel as a unit. Should they be received into fellowship on the face value of their profession of faith and then be trained in discipleship? Or should they, despite the evidence of God's working in their lives, be made to wait indefinitely? Western churches may have tried to demand too much of a new Christian. But by and large it would seem our failure has been that of expecting too little.

Certainly Jesus made clear that while in one sense salvation costs nothing, in another way its costs everything. He made certain specific demands of His followers when He called them to Himself. The watershed of the Gospels comes when Jesus takes His men to a mountain and asks them who they say He is. "You are the Christ, the Son of the Living God," answers Peter. And Jesus in effect replies, "Quite right, Peter, and you didn't make up that idea. God showed it to you. Now don't tell everyone yet because I have to go to Jerusalem to suffer, die, and rise again. And if you want to come after me you must be willing to die yourself! to put your own desires aside! to follow me! And if you're ashamed to acknowledge me before man, then I'll be ashamed to acknowledge you before God" (Cf. Matthew 16:13 f., and Luke 9:18 f.). He asked of them a conviction about Him, a commitment to Him, an open confession of Him before man.

Genuine commitment to Christ is not something man produces. We may pray for it, preach it, teach it, seek to demonstrate it, search for it. But ultimately faith in Christ is created by the Spirit of Christ just as Jesus told Peter it was not "flesh and blood" but the Father in Heaven who revealed to him who Jesus was. Jesus never hid His scars to win disciples, and we too must make the demands of discipleship clear.

A cousin of my wife's is the minister of an alive church on the growing edge of a Southern city. Sheer population growth could multiply their church membership, but he and the church officers won't have it that way. This young minister pays a personal call on every prospective member and explains what a Christian believes and how a Christian is expected to act. A West Point graduate and his wife began to attend this church and inquired about joining it. When the pastor had come to their home and talked with them the young man sat thoughtfully and then said, "I'd never heard it put like this. If that's what it means to become a Christian I'm not ready." For several months they continued to attend the church, and then one day the man called the pastor over and said, "Before I wasn't ready. I had no idea really what this Christian business was all about. I thought it was just joining the organization. Thank you for telling it like it is! Now I'm prepared truly to be Christ's man!"

It's also essential that the church be able to give a convincing demonstration of fellowship in Christ. This is especially true in this day of depersonalization when, as Paul Tournier remarks: "The more we fill our universe with machines, the more important it is that we treat each other as persons." Four hundred thousand young people went to the Woodstock festival in Bethel, New York. Psychoanalyst Rollo May said the event "showed the tremendous hunger, need and yearning for community on the part of youth."

Can these people find in your church and mine the thing that drove them to Max Yasgur's farm, the real belonging they were seeking? One minister I'm told calls new members of his church new "accounts." God forgive us if this is how we regard people. Our churches should be genuine "Bethels," where people are accepted and known as persons, whatever their bank account, the color of their skin, or the length of their hair. If any church is open only to the young, or only to bankers, or only to workers, or only to blacks, or only to whites, it ceases to be Christ's church and becomes a religious club. One night at the Billy Graham New York Crusade I looked down the row where I was sitting on the platform. On one side of me was a black friend and an Italian friend. On the other side was a Jewish Christian. And I thought, this is what the church should be: the place where black is beautiful and brown is beautiful and white is beautiful—in Christ!

Travelers to East Berlin know that Karl Marx Allee, the main street, is designed as a "demonstration" of what the new Communist society someday supposedly will be. Well, God intends that in our relationships with each other in the church of Christ we should be an authentic advance demonstration of what life in God s kingdom is going to be!

Then we also must understand that the whole church has a mission for Christ. By loving fellowship and compassionate service and patient suffering, and by sharing the good news of the Gospel, every Christian has a responsibility to make Christ known. Witness is not the task only of certain specialists. Kenneth Strachan's well-known study of the fastest growing movements in Latin America—the Communists, the Jehovah's Witnesses, the Pentecostal Churches—concludes that the common factor is their ability to mobilize their entire membership for the continuous propagation of their beliefs.

At the Leysin conference on "saturation evangelism," representatives of various churches and movements in the United States and overseas that had experienced outstanding evangelistic effectiveness pooled their discoveries. And again they, too, came to the conclusion that the mobilization and training of the church membership for outreach was an absolutely essential factor. Here is a key question for our day. Are we really serious enough about sharing our faith to come to real grips with this issue? Will we make in our churches whatever radical changes are necessary to mobilize Christians for continuous outreach?

Let me make several specific suggestions at this point. If our churches are to become committed, caring, witnessing fellowships then it will take at least the following things.

1. A revolution in our patterns of ministry. All of us—pastors, teachers, evangelists, and laymen—are going to have to understand that the church cannot afford to be made up of many spectators who pay to watch a few specialists do the work. We in the clergy must see that we are not to do all the work. We are coaches. Our

job is to build a team, starting with the leadership of our churches.

What I am saying here is a commonplace. But the thing that concerns me is how few churches are doing anything about it. How many churches have a specific training program to teach their people how to give away their faith? How many ministers are choosing twelve men as Jesus did, or even one or two, and equipping them for this work? How many laymen are actually insisting that their pastor turn over some of his tasks to others in order that he may give them this kind of training?

The Coral Ridge Presbyterian Church in Fort Lauderdale, Florida, is one church that has operated on precisely this principle. It is now one of the fastest growing churches in America. As Jim Kennedy, the minister of the church, tells it, the original days of his church did not exactly spell success. Within a few months of his going there as pastor the membership had actually dropped from 45 to 17. The discouraged Kennedy graphed this trend and estimated that he had two months left before the church closed or he quit the ministry!

At this point a friend invited him to be the visiting evangelist for a church in Georgia. Ignoring the irony of a failing pastor being asked to serve as an evangelist, Kennedy accepted the invitation, mainly to seek temporary escape from his problems. During his week in Georgia, however, the host pastor introduced him to a whole new concept of personal evangelism. He took Kennedy with him from house to house and demonstrated an effective way of leading people to Christ. Kennedy went back determined to put what he had learned into practice. Initially, his attempts were a failure. But finally he gained confidence and began to see people respond to the Gospel as he visited them in their homes.

Eventually he realized that the job was too big for him and that he needed the help of his people. So he gave them a series of training classes and sent them out. The whole effort fizzled; his discouraged workers quit. Finally, says Kennedy, he recognized his mistake. He himself, with all his years of theological training and all the books he had read, had been unable to win people to Christ until his pastor friend actually took him out and showed him how to do it. And here he was expecting his people to do it simply on the basis of a few classes. It was like trying to teach people to become pilots while they sit in a classroom. Ten, twenty, or even a hundred hours of classroom instruction will not teach people to fly an airplane. Only as they go up in the plane with an experienced instructor do they learn.

Acting on this insight, Jim Kennedy selected a few of his key laymen at a time. He took them with him and let them watch him in action. Then he turned over the responsibility of talking to the people they were visiting to the laymen under his supervision. Soon this one-to-one training made a difference, with noticeable results.

Today the Coral Ridge Presbyterian Church has a membership of close to 2000. At the beginning of each year they set as a prayer goal the number of people they hope to win to Christ that year. It is quite realistic to expect this goal will be reached. Their training program is continuing. For four months in the fall and in the spring experienced workers each choose two new people and take them visiting with them once a week for three months. Classroom instruction is also given. During the fourth month the trainees lead the evangelistic conversation in the homes as their supervisors watch. Then, during the next training period, they in turn each take two others. A clinic on evangelism held each February in the church attracts hundreds of pastors and laymen from throughout the United States. Yet the "secret" of Coral Ridge is very simple. They are simply following the basic pattern of Jesus, who took twelve men with Him and taught them by personal demonstration.

2. A revolution is also needed in the structures of our church life. Jesus preached to the great crowds; He also, as we have seen, poured His life into twelve men. In a mass society I believe there will be an increasing place for mass evangelism. The 400,000 young people who turned up at the Woodstock festival showed that mass gatherings make people pay attention. But a simultaneous emphasis will have to be on small intimate fellowships or else people will get lost in the crowd.

Inter-Varsity Christian Fellowship recently made a study in depth of the effect size had on its college chapters. They found that once a campus group passed 30, there was actually a decrease in its outreach. A group of 50 or 100 was actually reaching fewer of their peers with the gospel than a group of 20 or 30. The reason was evident. In a smaller group everyone had a chance to participate. Deeper fellowship was possible because everyone was known to the others. Responsibility could not be hoisted onto a small group of leaders. But as the groups grew in size the sense of involvement was lost. Inter-Varsity is now aiming to restructure its chapters into small "action groups," with about ten students forming the core. These groups will communicate with each other and pray for each other, and come together periodically for help and resources the small groups don't have: Bible teaching, evangelistic addresses, apologetic lectures. But the main structure for fellowship and witness will be the smaller action cell.

Does this not point up a vital lesson for the churches? Small groups are providing a big answer. Of course, they are not cure-alls. In fact, without adequate spiritual leadership they can encounter serious problems. But I suggest that the church of the future may well be made up of many such small groups. They will pray and study and share their problems and encourage each other in witness and service. Some will be centered around homes and some will meet in businesses and offices and schools. Some will cluster around specific social tasks and some will be formed in the various subcultures of our society. One group might be made up of young couples; another of social workers; a third of Apollo astronauts; a fourth of retired folks; a fifth of converted hippies and motor bikers; a sixth of converted preachers! All would come together on the Lord's Day to break bread together, to sing joyous songs of celebration together, to listen together to God's Word, to share testimony of God at work through their lives. Then they would scatter for another week of witness.

3. A revolution is needed in our whole attitude toward organization, buildings, and communication in church life. The church that wants to be "with it," not in terms of some superficial relevance, but in terms of effective outreach, will be forced into some painful reexaminations in all of these areas.

Take the matter of church "organization." So far as I know, God puts no premium on inefficiency, and we must have organization of some kind. Yet no aspect of the Christian faith draws as many negative votes today as "organized religion," "structured

Christianity." Why should young people be so dead set against "organization" in the church when some of man's most fantastic feats—the Apollo moon flights, relief flights to Biafra, and massive immunization campaigns against polio—have been accomplished by "organization"? Why is organization "good" in such efforts but "bad" in the church? Part of this reaction may be due to the impersonal character that much organization takes on, with decisions made at the top, far removed from grassroots feelings. But the main cause of this disillusionment is probably that too often church organization itself has become the goal, rather than a means to reach the goal. While the space program machinery is goal-oriented, and subject to constant review and evaluation, so much church time seems to be spent spinning wheels that are going nowhere. Sensitive laymen, who in business are accustomed to hard decisions about what is really working and what is not, throw up their hands in dismay when they see programs which have long ago outlived their usefulness continued in the church for sentiment's or old time's sake.

If the Church has been called to glorify God by winning men to Christ, building them up in the faith, and sending them out to witness and serve, then surely periodic studies should be made to see if the organization is serving these ends or serving itself. At least once in every decade every church should do as the North Avenue Presbyterian Church in Atlanta does. It should commission a group to restudy and pray through the mission and the mission field of the church—its responsibility to its membership, to the unevangelized, to the city on its doorstep, and to the world at large—and to reshape its program toward these goals. At least once a year the leadership of the church should meet to pray and plan together to decide under the guidance of the Holy Spirit goals for the year, and only then should programs be fashioned to meet those goals. Then if momentum lags the cure becomes not a matter of flogging a dead horse but of recapturing the original vision!

Killarney Baptist Church in Calgary, Alberta, has been struggling through a revolutionary change in its organization. Under the leadership of its pastor, Robert Roxburgh, they have been seeking to discover how the "irrelevant church," one isolated from its audience and actually organized *against* its goals, can be renewed. Roxburgh has produced a small handbook, *Pattern for Change*, which tells of their struggles and victories. He insists that a key to church renewal is making a distinction between organization (the church compared to a town, for example) and organism (the church seen as a family). His insight is worth quoting:

The Church that is an organism will give priority of emphasis [to] the goals; organization and plans will be of little or no significance at any given moment and where organization, always at a minimum, must be had, it is subject to change to suit the conditions . . . Further, the Organism church will create Christians who do not derive satisfaction from their church standing (meetings, etc.) but from their growth toward Biblical standards such as . . . "Am I personally sharing my faith? Do I love and create love? Do I invite lonely and needy families to my home? Do I train other Christians in the faith? Am I being drawn closer to Christ? Have I learned more of the Bible this year and put some of its profoundest precepts into practice? Am I initiating new ideas for expressing the Kingdom values in my community? Do I give to the poor and needy?

Roxburgh contrasts two concepts of the church in the following outline:

ORGANIZATION	ORGANISM
CHURCH TODAY	CHURCH TOMORROW
EFFECT ON GROUP LIFE	
1. Highly organized	1. Minimal organization
2. Ministry performed by agencies	2. Ministry by individuals in community
3. Much effort to maintain organization	3. Little organizational maintenance
4. Means and methods have priority	4. Values given priority
5. Status through position	5. Status related to value accomplishment
6. Effectiveness seen in terms of money, statistics, buildings, etc.	6. Effectiveness seen in terms of implementing community goals

RESULTS

Members are introduced into the organization and are guided into how to become good institutional church-goers	Members are introduced into the vibrant Christian community and are helped into growing in the values of the New Testament and of the community
Lots of deadwood in the membership	Active membership
Vagueness about commitment	Specific goals and awareness of commitment
Societal and not Biblical conformity	Conformity to Christ and the New Testament*

We must also have a revolutionary reevaluation of church buildings. As in the case of organization, there is no question that church buildings of some kind are necessary and useful. The question is whether buildings, too, may not become an end in themselves and be twisted from instruments into idols. Jesus seemed to express some feeling along this line when the disciples once pointed out to Him the magnificient temple buildings in Jerusalem. He responded, "You see all these, do you not? Truly, I say to you, there will not be left here one stone upon another, that will not be thrown down" (Matthew 24:2). That launched Him into a discussion of future events both near at hand and at the end of time, and of the kind of people His followers would have to be. Men, not mausoleums or monuments, were His preoccupation. Until recently American churches spent about a billion dollars a year on church buildings, many of which stand idle much of the time. There can be no question but that this so-called "edifice complex" has saddled some churches with huge debts that have diverted time, money, and attention away from evangelism, missions, and service.

In Brazil there is a fast-growing church that has developed from a moderate Pentecostal evangelistic movement known as "Brazil in Christ." A short time ago I met Levy Tavares, one of the three pastors of the mother congregation of this group in São Paulo. In

*This chart was adapted from material jointly prepared by the National Association of Evangelicals and the Wheaton College Department of Christian Education.

addition to serving as evangelist-minister of this church (which also has a teaching and an administrative minister), Levy is a congressman, representing several million persons and commuting weekly between Brasilia and São Paulo to fulfill his dual role. This charismatic young pastor told me the fascinating story of this movement, which has eighty-plus congregations in São Paulo to care for the converts of their evangelistic services. A lay pastor is appointed and a branch church formed for every hundred new Christians. The mother church has a building designed to seat 25,000 or more persons. Twice a month it is filled as their people come together from all parts of the city for a gigantic joint assembly. On alternate Sundays they meet in their own local areas under the guidance and leadership of their trained lay pastors.

That kindled my imagination. What if that pattern could be adapted throughout the world in the future. Instead of an expensive plant being built for each congregation, local fellowships of a church could either rent existing facilities or put up a relatively inexpensive multipurpose structure. Regularly these units would come together to a central meeting place, whether rented or owned, to praise and pray together; at other times they would meet in their local areas. This would free the "full-time" ministers to fulfill the particular gifts God has given each. Some would concentrate on preaching, some on teaching, some on counseling individuals, some on administration, dividing their time as overseers among the various congregations.

Lest you think that this is only the pipe dream of a traveling evangelist who doesn't know the facts of church life, let me report that a far-seeing denominational executive has already seriously made such a proposal. He approached a developer friend of mine, who is planning to build a major sports complex in his city, and said that he felt the waste of money on duplicated buildings came close to being sinful. Would it not be possible, he mused, for the churches of his denomination in that city to build a kind of coliseum that they could use on Sundays while renting it out on weekdays for sports and other activities? While his idea may never be implemented in that city, at least it set my friend, who is an active leader in his own church, to thinking of all the space they had that was never used. He had a conference with his minister and eventually their property was made available for free use by a variety of service organizations that needed space.

Communication within the average church is also due for a revolution. It may well be true that the church is the "last bastion of one-way communication" in our age, with the pulpit six feet above criticism. On the one hand the church in our day needs to recover a sense of the power and authority of preaching. But on the other hand we need to do away for good with the idea that the pastor always speaks (but never listens), or that only he speaks (never the layman). Fortunately that is a caricature, but still with enough truth to jab us where it hurts. One-way communication is not true to the Scriptures. Jesus had many question-and-answer sessions, and Paul dialogued as well as lectured. One-way communication is not in line with what the best studies of psychology and communication have taught us: that while lectures and addresses may inform, it is usually personal discussion that involves. And it is not true to the genius of our age, with its emphasis as much if not more on "sharing" as on "telling." Actually, one-way communciation, standing by itself, has always been out of date.

There is always likely to be a key place for mass communication in meetings, or on radio and television. The great crusades of Billy Graham and the more modest ones of other evangelists and the millions they have reached prove this to be true. But it's sometimes overlooked that even in the Billy Graham Crusades there is perhaps as much emphasis placed on personal contact and small group sessions as on the big meetings. Thousands of counselors are trained to have individual conversation with those who respond to the evangelist's appeal, and Bible study cell group leaders are recruited by the hundreds for the follow-up program.

In many of the Crusades conducted by Graham associate evangelists, radio "hot-line" programs have proved to be an invaluable means of penetrating a community. The evangelist is interviewed and then the audience actually voices their comments and questions on the air. One sometimes feels that there, even more specifically than in the mass meetings, the good news of Jesus can be related to the real issues facing real people. Similarly "rap sessions," as the students call them, open people to really listen.

In many of our Crusades student leaders at the various high schools, few of them committed Chistians, are invited to a reception. After a song and a very brief talk their questions are invited. The discussion can go on for hours, and the feeling is again that genuine communication has "happened." Often young people who would otherwise never have been interested subsequently attend a Crusade program and hear the Christian message with a new openness. Local churches can easily achieve the same end by feedback sessions in which questions the pastor's sermon has raised are fielded.

In the hill country of central Texas there is a retreat center known as Laity Lodge. It takes some effort to arrive there, for one must drive for miles through bleak country, turn onto a rough ranch road, drop into a valley, drive into the damned-up river, turn left, and keep going right in the river water for a mile or more! Those who have troubled to make the trip have found it worthwhile, for at Laity Lodge, spearheaded by lay leader Howard Butt, Jr., a unique concept of Christian communication has developed. Throughout the summer months a group of thirty to forty couples arrives each Sunday for an intensive five and a half days of encounter with Jesus Christ, His Spirit and His people. The first part of the day is given over to basic Bible study, and the Word of God is opened and taught for an hour or more. Then a trained psychiatrist, psychologist, or counselor speaks on some aspect of understanding one's self, personality dynamics, and group relationships. Finally, each person meets for an hour and a half with the *same* small group each day to discuss what he has heard and how it affects his own situation and struggle. The evening session is a time for inspiration and teaching on Christian beliefs.

Some of us who have shared in this experience feel that an exciting pattern has emerged that speaks to the whole Church. Many other conferences have focused either on Bible study, or on psychology, either on addresses or on group discussions. Here these elements are brought together in what can be—provided all the leadership is Bible-based and Christ-centered—a dynamic combination. Too often people have heard the Bible expounded but have not understood themselves well enough to apply it. Or else they have heard their problems analyzed but have found no spiritual resources for change. The Laity Lodge format is an encounter in which people can first hear God's plan for them, then be helped to see themselves as they are, and then by God's grace talk and pray these things through with other believers until they become real in their lives! The old custom of "praying through" has disappeared in most churches and evangelistic meetings, and the loss is great. Perhaps Laity Lodge is blazing a trail to recovery! A similar pattern could be tried in many churches in place of a Sunday morning routine that has gone stale. And saints might come alive!

At the U.S. Congress on Evangelism in Minneapolis, Richard Halverson made the strong point that genuine evangelism can only grow out of the seedbed of real Christian fellowship. "Community," he said,

is the matrix of mission. A congregation without community cannot fulfill its evangelistic mission, whatever is done to exhort or train. Conversely, when a congregation is spiritually healthy—that is, committed to Jesus Christ and to each other and constrained by a selfless concern for all men—evangelism will occur spontaneously, effortlessly, continuously, effectively . . . if we should lay aside momentarily our conventional views for the purpose of rediscovering what the New Testament says about evangelism, we would probably be surprised at the few references to the subject as such. We would find it treated, not as a task to be done, a department of church life (which we have made it in) not even as the primary role of the Church. Rather, evangelism is something that is happening all the time when the church is truly community, truly in fellowship, truly renewed and renewing.

Halverson is dead right. God's revolutionary Gospel has not lost its power. But unless we can revolutionize the structures of our churches we will bottleneck this Gospel and God will choose other channels.

11 A TIME TO ACT

J. B. Phillips entitled his paraphrase of the Book of Acts, *The Young Church in Action*, which signifies God's revolutionary power released through a revolutionary community in revolutionary action. Luke opens the Book of Acts by saying, "In the first book . . . I have dealt with all that Jesus began to do and teach" (Acts 1:1). He implies that Jesus continued "to do and teach" through those He left behind. This dynamic combination of deed and word characterized the apostles. Their words acted and their actions spoke. Acts is full of action verbs: they prayed, they spoke, they healed, they gave their testimony, they sold their goods, they went about preaching.

A frequent debate today concerns the "vertical" and the "horizontal"; or which comes first, getting right with God or getting right with man. Is this really the core of our problem? Are we not more in danger of being paralyzed in the wrong relationship between our speaking and our acting?

"Be doers of the word and not hearers only," James tells us. Our words must be matched with our deeds and our deeds with our words. God will judge us by whether we let our convictions be translated into revolutionary action.

This must begin with witnessing where we are ("in Jerusalem") and doing what we already know how to do. Then we can move on to new places and new ways. If we as Christians become obedient in doing what God has already told us to do, the new light and new ideas we are looking for might be quicker in coming!

Revolutionary action in evangelism will mean breaking some new ground. It will mean acting with other Christians from other churches. Our task is to confront everyone with the Gospel, and no one church can accomplish that task. Think what it would mean in your neighborhood if the Baptist and the Presbyterian and the

Lutheran and the other churches sent out teams of visitors to say, "We've come from all these churches to tell you of our one Lord and to ask you to receive Him into your life and follow Him in whichever of our churches He leads you!" As it was recorded of the early Church, "They had all things in common" and "None of them lacked anything." When Christians pool their resources they find that God multiplies them!

Revolutionary action in evangelism involves far-seeing and creative use of the mass media. Our Christian history has for too long shown us as bringing up the rear. Within our grasp are tools of communciation that God has made available to us, which now make it possible as never before to preach the Gospel to all nations. To be sure, the mass media are not a magic answer to all evangelistic problems as some seem to believe. Some studies indicate that communication through the mass media tends to confirm already held beliefs rather than to change them. The media must be used with sensitivity, with an awareness of the audience, and never as a substitute for personal contact. Yet God, Who in His careful planning had Roman roads ready to speed along the message of the first Christians and printing available to spread Reformation truth, now holds out to us new breakthroughs.

Edward Lindaman, a former aerospace executive and now president of Whitworth College, points out the potential of space "colonies" as communication relay points. By 1985, he predicts, orbiting craft will be capable of broadcasting radio and television programs directly to earth. While signals that originate on earth are limited in their coverage, programs broadcast from space will go directly to the receiving set. "Geophysical and political boundaries," he says, "will not exist. With three such stations orbiting the earth every nation on earth can be reached—without interference from any one on the ground, except the owner of the receiving set." Are Christians planning now to grasp this opportunity in fifteen years?

Something of the revolutionary potential of the media was demonstrated in the spring of 1970 in Dortmund, Germany. There in the heart of the industrial Ruhr, Billy Graham preached the Christian message for eight nights. Typical of Graham Crusade meetings were the crowds that jammed the 13,000-seat Westfalenhalle night after night. But something new had been added, a multilingual closed-circuit system that transformed the Dortmund effort into a massive trans-European outreach. Tens of thousands of people saw the evangelist nightly on large screens in 35 different cities, ranging from Tromso, Norway (330 miles north of the Arctic Circle), to Geneva, Switzerland, from Chatham, England, to Zagreb, Yugoslavia.

As a German interpreter translated for Dortmund and the other German cities, simultaneous translation was being given in at least six other languages. The total nightly audience averaged over 100,000 persons. "Never before," commented Billy Graham, "have we tried to reach so many people in so many countries at the same time by TV. This week I have preached to more people in person than in any previous week of my life." Altogether the Euro 70 Crusade was a thought-provoking reminder that revolutionary evangelism, in the name of the God Who made heaven and earth, who placed a human spirit in a body of clay, must combine the spiritual and the technological.

Revolutionary action in evangelism will mean taking the message to people where they are. Far too many of our evangelistic efforts fall flat because they take place in the church building. According to an old saying, the church should be "in the world but not of it." It can also be said that evangelism should always be *of* the church but not *in* it!

At a recent gathering Dr. Edward V. Hill, minister of the Mt. Zion Baptist Church in Los Angeles, gave a brilliant analysis of the evangelistic situation in the contemporary black churches. According to Dr. Hill, the black churches have put little emphasis on going outside the churches to reach the lost. They just expected their people to come to church. And as he humorously pointed out, until twenty or thirty years ago, if a black man did not come to church, you just "knew that some white fellow had been fooling around with him!" Dr. Hill pleaded for evangelistic movements to share their tools and the know-how of evangelism, for as he said, "for the first time we no longer have crowds seeking Christ; we must seek them." What Dr. Hill says of the black church is also true of the white church. We need to move from a "come" to a "go" mentality.

Jesus went where the people were. He preached on farms, by the roadside, in boats, and at dinner parties in the homes of sinners, and those who are really touching people for Christ are largely following His pattern. Thus Billy Graham goes on the Mike Douglas and Johnny Carson shows to make "sinner contact."

Bill Iverson, a young pastor in Newark, leaves his pulpit and buys a lunch counter across from an inner city high school and fries hamburgers in order to reach the kids who would not come to his church. Inner-city block parties have now become an important part of his work, which has developed into the "Cross Counter Ministry." A street is blocked off. Fried chicken is served and people sing and eat together. In a dramatic presentation given of the Gospel a man is chained to a wall and several keys are handed up. One is labeled "black power"; another "green power." Neither can open the lock. Finally a key is handed up called "love power" and the man is freed. He then turns to the crowd and tells them how the love of Christ has set him free.

In Los Angeles Arthur Blessitt has opened a "gospel night club" called "His Place." Twenty-four hours a day, seven days a week it is open to reach hippies and others on the Sunset Strip. Numerous striking conversions have taken place.

The local church must also take the Gospel "where the people are." Instead of paying to put a Sunday morning service on radio or television it might be more effective to take that same money and buy spots on the Saturday afternoon football game. That way there is assurance that at least some pagans are watching, and a 60-second spot announcement may get to them whereas they would certainly turn off a 30- or 60-minute program.

There is tremendous appeal in much of the special music done by church choirs, particularly at Christmas and Easter times. The trouble is the people who might be reached are not at church to hear it. What could be the impact if a choir, provided it is good enough, put on its program in a shopping mall instead of in the sanctuary of the church? Along with some well-chosen passages of Scripture and perhaps a distribution of the Christmas story in booklet form, a tremendous evangelistic impact could be made at Christmastime.

The traditional evangelistic meetings in local churches have often lost their impact precisely because the outsiders do not come to the service. Congregations might be well advised to rent a theater instead for the next series of evangelistic meetings. Alan Walker's Central Methodist Mission in Sydney, Australia, actually holds all its Sunday night services in a downtown theater, and almost every Sunday night there are conversions. Similarly, the Billy Graham film ministry has seen a great upsurge in conversions once the decision was made to show dramatic films in theaters rather than in churches.

Some have strongly criticized going to a "secular" or "worldly" scene to present the Gospel. It is difficult to see how this can be any more of a problem than buying time on a television station, renting an arena, or utilizing a printing press that might also be used for questionable purposes. The point is that this is where the people are.

Recently in our hometown we had a group of Christian folksingers visiting from Australia. Rather than putting on a program in a church we rented the local dinner theater on its off night. A group of Christian couples invited their friends and their teenage children. Many of them were nonbelievers and non–church attenders. They might never have gone to the church itself. But in a setting where they had had dinner and watched a play they were exposed in a powerful fashion to the reality of Jesus Christ. Surely this approach, if it *is* worldly, is so only in the sense that our Lord was worldly, for He came into the world to save sinners. He mixed with them and was criticized for it, but by seeking common ground He was able to win some over to His cause.

Revolutionary evangelism will mean taking the Gospel to revolutionary people. Most of our evangelism involves reaching the family and friends of those who are already Christians. Often these are middle-class respectable citizens. There is nothing wrong with this, for respectable middle-class citizens make up most of our population, and they need Christ. Anthropologists have suggested that in most cultures the upper class censures information, the lower class receives information, while the middle class conveys information. Therefore it is strategically important to reach the middle class for Christ as well as it is spiritually essential not to neglect them. But meanwhile we have to think also about the subcultures.

Who is reaching the hippies in your town? the student radicals? the ghettos? the intellectuals? the motorcycle crowd? the rock crowd? the swingers in apartments? Relating to these people will mean praying that God will call some Christians to be missionaries to these subcultures just as we send missionaries to Brazil and Thailand. They will have to be sent expressly to make contact, to learn the language and customs of the "natives," and to identify with them as Christ identified with us.

The Young Life organization has illustrated this kind of "incarnational" evangelism with the youth culture. Instead of expecting young people to come to a religious setting, they release their workers to go where young people are. Young Life staff people will stay around the high school, around the athletic field and the gym, and around the drug store. They learn the local language and cultures and habits. A great deal of time will be spent simply making friendships and demonstrating a personal interest in the lives of the young people. When the of friendship has been built that crosses any generation gap.

Apartment dwellers are notoriously difficult for modern churches invitation is finally given to attend a Young Life meeting, a bridge to contact. In high-rise apartments doormen bar the way to salesmen and preachers. Appeals to attend church are met with indifference, particularly on the part of young people who live in apartment complexes that cater to their set. Perhaps a church might make contact by praying that God would choose one or two young couples who would take it as their evangelistic mission to go and live in an apartment house. They would have to be especially trained for this ministry so that they might first make friends and then perhaps start a Bible study in their apartment, eventually building a "house church" there for people who've resisted every effort to get them "to go to church." In such cases the church will have to learn to go to them.

Revolutionary evangelism will also mean earning the right to speak to lives bruised and battered by social upheaval. Can the Gospel win a hearing, for example, in the urban ghettos, where militants wear buttons saying, "I hate Jesus," and where the Black Muslims say that Christianity is "whitey's" religion?

I asked this question of several men who are giving their lives to the Gospel in New York's ghettos. Each of them agreed that love is the key. One said, "It's not until love is felt that the message is heard." Another commented, "The secular city men left the message back home. Evangelicals kept the beautiful message but did nothing about it. The people in the inner city have heard so many raps they are disenchanted. We have to love people without strings attached and give our message off the springboard of involvement. This is the rap that will be heard." A black leader, when asked what he regarded as the first priority of inner-city evangelism, replied quickly, "a balanced diet of love for all people. The key to being heard is honesty. People have to feel (1) this man believes what he is saying; (2) this person is concerned about me."

Evangelism must be love with flesh on, what Bill Milliken who works on Manhattan's East Side calls "tough love." We must echo Amos as well as Paul, Micah as well as Peter. Our message has got to combine the prophets, who called for repentance and justice, with the apostles, who called for repentance and faith in Jesus Christ. Christians involved in the search for racial and economic justice may be door-openers for evangelism. This isn't to say that social involvement is only a gimmick for evangelism. Rather, as Carl Henry said at the World Congress on Evangelism in Berlin, "The Bible dictates for us a double concern: that men may receive justification from God and that they may have justice from their fellow men."

At the U.S. Congress on Evangelism in Minneapolis in September 1969, one of the speakers humorously commented, "Evangelism and social action have been like the old steamboat: when it whistled it couldn't move and when it moved it couldn't whistle!" Thank God, it was obvious at that same Congress that evangelical Christians were being led by God to smash that false antithesis. Speaker after speaker underlined with conviction and passion that while social action and evangelism are not to be identified, neither can they be completely separated. In a similar vein, at the Latin American Congress on Evangelism in Bogota in November 1969, Dr. Samuel Escobar drew a standing ovation for his brilliant and penetrating addess on "The Social Responsibility of the Church." Dr. Escobar's message struck a beautiful biblical balance. Two of his statements will bear this out:

Our sermons and tracts urge the drunkards to leave their liquor, the thieves and delinquents to leave their bad ways, disobedient children to respect their parents. What does our message say to the exploiters of the Indians, the abuse of capitalists, to corrupt police, to dirty politicians? Isn't it a sin or an indication of sin to be comfortably indifferent in the face of the suffering of the masses of our continent?

Later he went on to point out,

Service is not evangelism. Men, whatever their social class, economic condition or political position, need to know that God loves them and that Christ offers them the way to return to God. Rich and poor, capitalist and worker, military and politician, all need to hear the call to repentance and faith. To proclaim the good news by preaching, personal testimony, literature and Bible distribution is always necessary, here and now, by every believer. But he who evangelizes has a different life. He is someone who has learned to serve. He is a living letter who shows forth the truth and the applicability of the message he proclaims. We can never separate the proclamation of the Gospel from the demonstration of that Gospel. They are different but both are indispensable.

To boil it down to its essence: As Christians we have to be concerned, both for love and justice. Love goes beyond justice, and only the saving and transforming power of Jesus Christ can produce this kind of real love. But love is not a substitute for justice, and since not all men are or will be converted to Christ, and since even we Christians have imperfect love, we have a responsibility to seek justice in society. A Christian politician who seeks to pass laws that create guidelines for justice is doing God's work just as truly as a Christian pastor who seeks to win the lost to Christ.

William Wilberforce was converted to Christ as a young man in England. Then God put within his heart a burning passion to abolish the slave trade, and he went on a campaign to wipe out that evil. He did this not only by preaching the Gospel but also by fierce debate and political action. He even joined Christian and non-Christian alike in this campaign.

There are those who think that while this may have been good enough in Wilberforce's day, or may work in "Christian" America or Britain, it is neither sufficient nor radical enough for our fast-moving day or for other cultures. A letter from a missionary to Brazil indicates quite the contrary. This young man has had a highly unusual and effective impact on the political leadership of a nation. He and his colleagues in Christian Leadership of Brazil operate on the principle that leaders themselves have more technical knowledge about their field than an outsider. What is needed for Christian action is not necessarily more technical knowledge, but Christ. Their goal is to introduce leaders to Jesus Christ and to trust that in fellowship with other leaders who know Him they may find the discernment and power of the Holy Spirit to exercise Christian responsibility. Acting not as a pressure group, but promoting Christian fellowship, prayer and the word of God, they have seen specific concrete results.

For example, a Brazilian dairymen's association wanted to stop the free distribution of dry milk by foreign countries to school children in a certain state. They demanded an immediate cutoff, insisting that otherwise the schools would not buy their milk and the economy would be cut back. Here was a tangled problem, involving economic development on the one hand and the needs of thousands of small children on the other. The problem was brought up in the leadership prayer group. Present was a top political leader who decided, after meditation, that he would not support the dairymen's request. He would resign rather than be a party to a measure to deprive the children of their milk. And he proposed a new bill, eventually accepted, by which the milk would be cut off only in stages. Hence the dairymen would have to wait a little longer but would still be able to develop without unfair competition, and the children would continue to receive the free milk until the state was prepared to purchase it.

On another occasion a congressman brought to the group a meditation on "Blessed are the peacemakers." Out of the discussion that day, which revolved around the problem of nuclear war, an agreement was reached to have Brazil sign a treaty, with other

Latin American nations, to prohibit the construction of atomic weapons on their continent. Again the men prayed about the terrible housing situation in the country. Individually and together they were able to begin a national housing project to provide homes for tens of thousands who had been living in squalor and filth. In a similar fashion, they prayed about the poverty in the northeast sector of Brazil. Out of their concern, in part, came a law permitting businesses and individuals to invest tax-free in industry for that section in an effort to spur the economy.

It should be emphasized, cautions the missionary, that the Christian Leadership organization did none of this. It exerted an influence on those who did. Again, the revolutionary motivation of the Gospel led to the *right* kind of compassionate action!

Recently I was moved by the story of a number of churches in Fort Wayne, Indiana, that had become involved in rehabilitating housing. They would buy a house in a deteriorating area, renovate it, and then offer it for sale at a price that was within the means of poor families. One of the men who is involved in this project said, "We are not just concerned about housing, we want to see people come to Christ. And personally, I see no contradiction between kneeling down in prayer with a man as I lead him to Christ, which I've done many times, and kneeling down to nail linoleum on the floor so he can have a decent house to live in!" That's the combination of word and deed and action that rings true.

Again, compassionate social action should not be confused with evangelism; neither should it be separated from it. Like love and marriage, they go together!

Please note carefully: I am not saying that we can build a perfect world by our efforts. We can make some things better, but the new world will not come until Christ returns. Nor am I saying that the Church should stop giving priority to evangelism and become a political lobby. What I am saying is that God wants to give through our lives as Christians a kind of preview, an advance demonstration of the love and peace and justice that will mark His eternal kingdom. Then, when from a platform of love in action we ask men to be reconciled to God, the Church's message will sound with the ring of truth.

12 HE SHALL OVERTURN!

When Admiral Peary was exploring at the North Pole, he started out early one morning with his dog team to drive toward the north. At the end of the day he made camp and took a bearing on his latitude. To his surprise he found that apparently he was farther south than he had been in the morning. He was baffled until eventually he found that he was actually on a gigantic ice floe that was being pulled toward the south faster than his dog team could pull him toward the north.

Sometimes it seems as if our civilization is also on a gigantic ice floe. Great unseen spiritual and moral forces are pulling us back faster than we can move ahead. One step forward seems to be followed by one step back. Are we making progress? The answer would appear to be yes *and* no, that things are getting better and worse at the same time.

Can we then talk realistically about "changing the world"? Is the vision of a "new world in the morning" simply a pipe dream?

In the Bible one finds again and again the picture of a new world, envisioned in a splendor that outrivals the dreams of any revolutionary. Many hundreds of years before Christ, Isaiah peered into the future and saw a day when God would "judge between the nations . . . and they shall beat their swords into plowshares and their spears into pruning hooks; nation shall not lift up sword against nation, neither shall they learn war any more" (Isaiah 2:4).

Similarly John in his Revelation foresees "a new heaven and a new earth," a time when God's dwelling would be with men. He will dwell with them and they shall be his people and God himself will be with them; he will wipe away every tear from their eyes and death shall be no more, neither shall there be mourning nor crying nor pain any more, for the former things have passed away" (Revelation 21:1, 3–4). And John heard the one who sat upon the throne say, "Behold, I make all things new" (Revelation 21:5). There will be a new world in the morning! Utopia is coming! That is the vision of the Bible.

Yet alongside this vision the Bible has a very realistic view of history. In fact, a philosophy of history is one of the distinctive ideas the Bible teaches us. According to the biblical writers, history is neither an aimless cycle nor a riddle without meaning. It is like an arrow shot toward a mark; it has a beginning and an ending, and it has a target toward which God is moving everything.

Indeed, if we study the Bible carefully we are not surprised if the world seems to get better and worse simultaneously. This pattern is exactly what is predicted! The clue to this strange quirk of history is found in a profound story that Jesus Christ told two thousand years ago. A farmer, He said, went out and planted wheat in his field. While he was sleeping along came an enemy and planted weeds, or tares, in the same field. Wheat and weeds sprouted up together, but the farmer said to his hired hands, "Leave them alone until the harvest. Then we will separate the wheat from the weeds and burn up the weeds with fire" (cf. Matthew 13:24–30).

"Our world is like that," said Jesus in effect. "God made the world, and He made it good. But the enemy of God, the devil, came along and sowed weeds. He tempted man to rebel against God. Ever since everything that has happened in human history has been affected by the weeds of sin." In other words, Jesus explained that we could expect to see what we are seeing! Good will get better and evil will get worse. And this will happen until the end of time when at the last day God will separate the wheat from the tares and will judge and destroy evil once and for all.

Those who understand this teaching of Jesus are realistically prepared when they set out to change things. They expect no permanent solution, no permanent answer to humanity's problems this side of Christ's return. Instead they understand that a spiritual revolution is needed in every generation. Conflict between good and evil is a characteristic of this age. Jesus never predicted a perfect and peaceful world system to emerge before He comes back. Nor did He hold out the hope that everyone would be converted. The good news of God's rule, He told His disciples, would be preached in all nations (Mark 13), a prophecy that is very close to fulfillment today! Yet before His return He warned there would be wars, unbelief, a falling away from faith, troubles, and persecutions (cf. Matthew 24). Paul foresaw the "lawless one" released from all restraint before the coming of Christ (2 Thessalonians 2:7–8), and told Timothy that wicked men would "make progress from bad to worse" (2 Timothy 3:13)! That is the kind of progress we don't like to think about!

Yet as believers we need not despair. Conflict will not go on endlessly. History is moving toward the great showdown, the "25th hour." Toward the end the struggle will grow stronger. Evil will appear to break through all restraints. But the climax will come in Christ's personal return. "I will come again," He promised (John 14:3). That is, in David Livingstone's terms, the word of a gentlemen of the highest order! He will return!

The future is Christ's. "For God has allowed us to know the secret of His plan and it is this: He purposes, in His sovereign will, that all human history should be consummated in Christ, that everything that exists in Heaven or earth shall find its perfection and fulfillment in Him" (Ephesians 1:9–10, Phillips trans.).

Cornelius Ryan wrote two fascinating accounts of World War II in Europe. *The Longest Day* details D–Day, when the Allied forces landed on Normandy and gained a foothold in Nazi Europe. His second work, *The Last Battle*, recounts the fall of Berlin. In one sense the war was over when Normandy's beaches were invaded; a decisive and fateful blow to Hitler's forces had been struck. Yet it was only after months had passed, fierce battles had been fought, and tens of thousands of men killed that Germany surrendered. Jesus' first coming, the divine D–Day, was God's decisive invasion of history.

When Jesus hung on a cross and died it was truly history's "longest day," for what Jesus did in dying for our sins and defeating evil stretched backward and forward into eternity. Jesus' second coming will be V–Day! He will come in "glory and great power." The last battle will be fought! "Then comes the end, when he delivers the kingdom to God the Father after destroying every rule and every authority and power. For He must reign until he has put all his enemies under his feet. The last enemy to be destroyed is death" (1 Corinthians 15:24–26). Conflict will come to a climax and climax will issue in a crisis of judgment. There will be, as Jesus taught in His story, a separating or a dividing. Justice will be done; goodness rewarded; and evil will reap its punishment. The redeemed will be welcomed into God's eternal Presence, while the lost will face separation from God and eternal judgment (Matthew 25:46). In that day men will give glory to God in the highest and God will give peace to man on earth!

This hope of Christ's return is no escapist clause. It is not an out for Christian complacency, nor an alibi for noninvolvement. On the contrary, it is a spur to holiness, to evangelism, to obedience. It is a motivation to make God's work on earth our own, for Jesus told us in parable form to "occupy until I come" (Luke 19:13). Like Martin Luther we are to live and work as though Jesus Christ died yesterday, rose today, and is coming again tomorrow!

Once God invaded history in Jesus Christ to begin His revolution. Some day, perhaps sooner than we think, He will intervene and bring His revolution to completion, "making all things new." Now we stand between D–Day and V–Day. In this interim period we are called to repent and believe the Gospel, to follow Jesus our revolutionary leader, to preach His good news and practice His new life. We cannot make a perfect world, but we can by God's grace make some things different, and what we can do by God's grace we should do.

What a breathtaking vision we have seen! the sweep of a revolutionary God who is shaking all things, and releasing His revolutionary power through His revolutionary people in revolutionary action. Frankly, it makes me shrink back and ask how I can be a revolutionary for Christ when God's plan is so big and my strength is so small? I identify much more with Snoopy, daydreaming on top of his doghouse about fighting the Red Baron than I do with some daring revolutionary! I bow my head in shame when I contrast the tame Christian I am with the bold Christian I should be. And somehow I realize that when my life fails to meet God's revolutionary expectations it is not God who has failed. It is I who have failed to let the Holy Spirit, the master agent of God's strategy, have full control of my life.

I also realize that God's revolution is going to go on with or without me. But I don't want to get left behind. So this is my prayer:

LORD, START A REVOLUTION AND START IT IN ME!

And this seldom quoted verse from Ezekiel 21:27 gives us, I believe, God's sovereign answer:

"I WILL OVERTURN, OVERTURN, OVERTURN . . . UNTIL HE COMES WHOSE RIGHT IT IS: AND I WILL GIVE IT HIM!"

71 72 73 10 9 8 7 6 5 4 3 2

	DATE DUE		